The Language of Fashion

Linguistic Insights

Studies in Language and Communication

Edited by Maurizio Gotti,
Emeritus Professor, University of Bergamo,
(Italy)

Volume 293

PETER LANG
Bern · Berlin · Bruxelles · New York · Oxford

Annalisa Baicchi / Stefania Biscetti (eds.)

The Language of Fashion

Linguistic, Cognitive, and Cultural Insights

PETER LANG

Bern · Berlin · Bruxelles · New York · Oxford

Bibliographic information published by die Deutsche Nationalbibliothek
Die Deutsche Nationalbibliothek lists this publication in the Deutsche National-
bibliografie; detailed bibliographic data is available on the Internet
at ‹http://dnb.d-nb.de›.

Library of Congress Cataloging-in-Publication Data
A CIP catalog record for this book has been applied for at the
Library of Congress.

This volume has been financed by the Italian Ministry of University, Research and
Education, PRIN grant no. Prot. 2015TJ39LF.

ISSN 1424-8689   ISBN 978-3-0343-4428-9 (Print)
E-ISBN 978-3-0343-4609-2 (E-PDF) E-ISBN 978-3-0343-4610-8 (EPUB)
DOI 10.3726/b20106

© Peter Lang Group AG, International Academic Publishers, Bern 2022
bern@peterlang.com, www.peterlang.com

CONTENTS

ANNALISA BAICCHI / STEFANIA BISCETTI

Insights into the Language of Fashion.
By Way of Introduction

Fashion is a complex phenomenon that lends itself to a variety of approaches. It merges many aspects of society and human life, and as such it is the object of study in many fields of investigation, such as sociology, semiotics, and linguistics, to name a few. It has lately received an increasing amount of attention from cultural historians interested in the evolution of costume, at least judging from the number of books on the history of fashion and clothing published over the last seven years (Thompson Ford 2022; Thanhauser 2022; Cumming 2021; Tiramani et al. 2021; Edwards 2017; Rissman 2015; Cole and Deihl 2015).

Fashion constantly introduces innovation and changes our way of communicating our beliefs through apparel, and with its creativity it affects not only the clothes we wear, but also the terminology we use to talk about them. As a matter of fact, since change, innovation and mutability are key features of «the real vestimentary code», they are doomed to affect «the written vestimentary code or the terminological system» (Barthes 1983: 36).

Barthes's association of the verbal code with its lexical component is telling of the centrality that vocabulary has in linguistic research on fashion language. Neologisms, linguistic borrowing, false anglicisms (Gottlieb and Furiassi 2015; Lopriore and Furiassi 2015; Görlach (2001, 2002a, 2002b); Fischer and Pulaczewska 2008; Campos and Balteiro 2020) have been extensively investigated, possibly to the risk of overshadowing other phenomena pertaining to this type of specialised language.

This volume broadens its perspective to include contributions on the syntactic and morphological aspects of fashion language and accounts for the growing interest that the language of fashion has exerted on scholars from different scientific fields and theoretical persuasion.

It opens with **Louise Sylvester**'s chapter titled "The lexicalization of the idea of fashion in later medieval Britain". The author investigates the lexicalization of the notion of fashion in Britain in the later medieval period, and she examines the vocabulary relating to dress and textiles retrieved from three lexicographical resources: the database of the Lexis of Cloth and Clothing project; the *Bilingual Thesaurus of Everyday Life in Medieval England* (collected under the occupational domain of Domestic activities); and the *Historical Thesaurus of English*. The chapter takes three main features as diagnostics for the idea of fashion: (1) the number of lexical items within the subcategories of terms for garments and accessories, noting Wotherspoon's (1969) suggestion that if there is a high degree of semantic continuity in certain fields (i.e., a concentration of a large number of minutely distinguished words and even of synonyms) these fields may be cultural themes, and the recent innovations of lexicalization sparklines tool in the online *Historical Thesaurus* which allows users to see how categories grow and wane over time; (2) the frequency with which terms undergo shifts in sense; and (3) the rates at which terms became obsolete or were replaced, in particular by items borrowed from French. Through the accurate analysis of the resulting data, elements of dress that were particularly susceptible to changes in fashion have been isolated and compared to the garments and ways of wearing them that were discussed in contemporary discourses about clothing, including diatribes against fashion, which can be found in the histories, sermons, conduct literature, satirical verses, romances, and sumptuary laws, collected in Sylvester et al (2014).

In the chapter "Nominal constructs in fashion and costume: Names and Nouns as modifiers", **Silvia Cacchiani** concentrates on English terms and, more specifically, on nominal constructs (Booij 2010) with Noun or Name as modifiers, in the changing history of fashion and costume. Starting on the assumption that proper Names and appellative Nouns form prototypical categories with fuzzy boundaries (van Langendonck 2007; Van Langendonck and van de Velde 2016), she provides a qualitative investigation of a representative selection of terms manually gathered from encyclopaedic dictionaries, visual dictionaries, and landmark publications on the history of fashion. With great clarity the analysis shows that conceptual metonymy is a major determinant of the shift from the identifying and individualizing function of prototypical place and personal names to classifying uses as appellative nouns, also in reductions to simplexes (e.g. *Ascot tie/Ascot*). Additionally, considering the linking rule R in the composite structure, Cacchiani suggests that, firstly, the COMMEMORATIVE function (cf., e.g., Schlücker 2016) underlies CLASSIFY (Jackendoff 2010) in non-descriptive specifications, and, secondly, the shift to EPITHET (Breban 2018) and the TYPIFY function (Koptjevskaja-Tamm 2013) can be motivated metonymically whenever associative/emotive meanings and complex descriptions enter the picture, as in *Kelly bag/Hermès Kelly/Kelly*. Another observation concerns the potential for certain constructs and iconic products to retain their ability to convey complex descriptions, which is ultimately a matter of cultural and encyclopaedic knowledge (knowledge of brand, brand products, and style icons).

Dedicated to "Fashion-based (pseudo-)Anglicisms in Spanish women's fashion magazines", **Isabel Balteiro** considers the rapid advances and modernization of fashion, which sometimes make languages unable to cope with the rapid pace with which extralinguistic realities change, and English global recognition, prestige and appeal that lead other world languages to borrow and use English words, be these necessary or not. In particular, Spanish has been increasingly incorporating Anglicisms but also creating false or pseudo-Anglicisms which are equally loved and hated by language users and scholars, depending on their descriptive or prescriptive-purist approach to the language. These foreign English terms are most visible in the language of fashion, where they are highly appreciated and associated to prestige and "coolness". Based on a sample of over ten million words from internationally-recognized specialized fashion magazines, Balteiro focuses on the use of the English term 'fashion' itself in its nominal and non-nominal uses in Spanish, with the aim of identifying and describing the nominal and adjectival uses of fashion, which may be either directly taken from English in phrases or compounds.

Elisa Mattiello investigates the use of spatial particles in the formation of English compounds in fashion language in the chapter *"Underwear as overwear*: Spatial particles in English fashion compounds". Spatial particles such as *under, over,* or *out* are frequent compound constituents in English (Bauer et al. 2013), and some scholars even consider them "native locative prefixes" (e.g., Bauer et al. 2013) on account of their productivity in the formation of nouns such as *under-wear*, *overwear*, and *outfit*. Yet, some of these particles are also found in "prepositional compounds" (Bauer et al. 2013) derived by conversion from phrasal verbs, such as the nouns *push-up* and *pullover* obtained from the respective verbs. Her study examines a set of nominal compounds drawn from *Victoria's Secret* and *H&M* websites to inspect the relevance of spatial particles to the creation of English fashion terms. Fashion spatial compounds are rich in English, especially nominal compounds that exhibit a location-located semantic structure, such as *beach dress* and *topcoat* (Biscetti & Baicchi 2019). The research spe-cifically focuses on nominal compounds exhibiting spatial particles, as words related to clothes or accessories need to be located with respect to other garments (*underskirt*) or human body (*backpack*). Through accurate corpus analysis (COCA, Davies 2008), Mattiello provides a morphosyntactic and morphosemantic analysis of English fashion prepositional compounds, and categorises based on the notions of trans-parency, compositionality, headedness, productivity, and analogy. She has been able to show the relevance of spatial particles related to the vertical axis (*under*, *over*), which in fashion terminology have become productive compound constituents (Bauer 2001; Mattiello 2017).

"The Political Language of Fashion" is the research object of **Anna Romagnuolo**'s chapter, which explores political expressions, words, and turn of phrases inspired by fashion items, and coined or popularized, knowingly or unknowingly, by politicians and especially US president incumbents, elects and candidates. It is well known that clothes, accessories, and hairstyles have always conveyed more than a message of individual taste, in that they reflect social hierarchies of value, display individual and collective inclinations, reveal conscious or unconscious beliefs about identities, convey religious norms, social status, and personal experiences. However, in today's political world, affected by a global pandemic, economic stagnation, progressive deple-tion of raw materials and a rise of far right, populist, and authoritar-ian movements, they acquire an ever-increasing political voice. On closer scrutiny, fashion and politics are related and have always been so, despite the limited and only recent attention paid by scholars to their mutual influence. Not only do political choices impact garment production systems and buyers' spending, but they also respond to fashion trends. Fashion and style have always contained messages that have wider meaning than that implied by the wearer and that create a larger nonverbal discourse imbued with political significance. Many are the examples: from medieval, renaissance and early colonial sumptuary laws imposing restrictions on clothing, aimed at reinforcing social hierarchies, to modern customs duties on imports of textiles, from policies promoting sustainable cotton growth and recyclable clothing to fashion designers' engagement in political debates discussing the expression of racial and ethnic diversity in style and, conversely, the fight against cultural appropriation and colonization of the fashion industry, from hippies' experimentation with a natural and loose look as a form of protest against big corporations and restrictive societal norms to contemporary choices of wearing a pink pussy hat or a Covid-19 face protective mask to protest against or align with Trumpian attitudes and policies.

In her chapter entitled *"It's never 'just a trouser!'* Bipartite nouns as singulars in the language of fashion", **Stefania Biscetti** explores the grammatical and semantic aspects of bipartite garment nouns used as singulars in the language of fashion by focusing on the lexical item *trouser(s)*. The accurate analysis of the dataset, compiled with occurrences retrieved from *The Vogue Archive* (America), challenges two common claims: (1) bipartites are *pluralia tantum* nouns, i.e., occuring only in the plural, (since *trousers* has passed the same tests for countability that *scissors* failed (Allan 1980)); (2) bipartites can only express generic reference to type, model, or style when they are used as singulars (Wickens (1992); Payne & Huddleston (2002)), (since a few few cases were found of *trouser* being used in captions with specific, indexical reference to the item portrayed in the picture). The paper also challenges the claim about the iconic form-meaning relationship embodied by the plural form (*trousers*) (Wierzbicka 1988), since the use of the singular form *trouser* to refer to one leg of a pair of trousers was found to be cognitively grounded in the way of conceptualizing the human body (i.e., as two symmetrical halves) in this specific domain of human activity. This finding suggests that iconicity can also have a local, discourse-specific validity.

The volume closes with **Annalisa Baicchi**'s observations on "Clothes we dress in. The conceptualisation of fashion terms". The chapter starts from the assumption that language is the arena where patterns of experience, social interaction, and cognitive processes intertwine in dynamic and complex ways (Baicchi 2015). The study explores clothing lexemes and exemplifies how language conflates the perception of our body in the spatial extent as well as in the cultural space. The chapter inspects a dataset of English clothing terms retrieved from one of the most accredited dictionaries, *The Fairchild Dictionary of Fashion*, with a view to identifying the cognitive operations that motivate clothing terminology and to assessing the degree of conceptual complexity that those terms entail. The research is couched in Cognitive Linguistics and Cultural Linguistics. Relying on some core tenets such as categorisation and idealised cognitive models (Lakoff 1987), and cultural conceptualizations (Sharifian 2017), fashion lexemes are classified into the four categories of frames, embodied schemas, metonymy, and metaphor, as well as on cultural schemas and cultural categories. Along the gradient of complexity, embodied schemas-based compounds occupy at the lowest level of both conceptual and cultural complexity, while cultural or frame-based lexemes occupy the highest degrees.

We think that the original chapters in this volume provide interesting insights on the topics they explore, and we hope that they can contribute to advancing our understanding of the complex prismatic nature of fashion in its linguistic, cultural and cognitivist aspects.

Acknowledgements

Our heartfelt gratitude goes to the authors who kindly accepted our invitation to contribute to this volume, to Professor Maurizio Gotti, the Editor of the *Linguistics Insights* Series who kindly welcomed our editorial proposal, to Ulrike Döring who has generously assisted us in all steps of the publishing process, and to the excellent production team of Peter Lang.

The volume has been financed by the Italian Ministry of University, Research and Education, PRIN grant no. Prot. 2015TJ39LF.

References

Allan, Keith. 1980. Nouns and countability. *Language* 56(3): 541–567.

Baicchi, Annalisa. 2015. *Construction Learning as a Complex Adaptive System*. Dodrecht: Springer.

Barthes, Roland. 1983. *The Fashion System*. Berkley and Los Angeles: University of California Press.

Bauer, Laurie. 2001. *Morphological Productivity*. Cambridge: Cambridge University Press.

Bauer, Laurie, Rochelle Lieber, and Ingo Plag. 2013. *The Oxford Reference Guide to English Morphology*. Oxford: Oxford University Press.

Biscetti, Stefania and Annalisa Baicchi. 2019. "'Space oddity': What fashion terms can reveal about English and Italian cognitive systems". In Simona Segre Reinach (ed.), *The Culture, Fashion, and Society Notebook*. Milano/Torino: Pearson-Mondadori, 29–43.

Booij, Geert E. 2010. *Construction Morphology*. Oxford: Oxford University Press.

Cole, Daniel James and Nancy Deihl. 2015. *The History of Modern Fashion*. London: Laurence King Publishing.

Cumming, Valerie. 2021. *Understanding Fashion History*. London: Batsford.

Davies, Mark. 2008. *Corpus of Contemporary American English* (COCA). Available at https://corpus.byu.edu/coca/

Edwards, Lydia. 2017. *How to Read a Dress: A Guide to Changing Fashion from the 16th to the 20th Century*. London-New York: Bloomsbury Academic.

Fischer, Roswitha and Hanna Pułaczewska (Eds.). 2008. *Anglicisms in Europe. Linguistic Diversity in a Global Context*. Newcastle upon Tyne: Cambridge Scholars Publishing.

Gottlieb Henrik and Cristiano Furiassi (Eds.). 2015. *Pseudo-English: Studies on False Anglicisms in Europe*. Berlin: De Gruyter Mouton.

Görlach, Manfred. 2001. *A Dictionary of European Anglicisms*. Oxford: Oxford University Press.

Görlach, Manfred (Ed.). 2002a. *English in Europe*. Oxford: Oxford University Press.

Görlach, Manfred (Ed.). 2002b. *An Annotated Bibliography of European Anglicisms*. Oxford: Oxford University Press.

Jackendoff, Ray. 2010. "The ecology of English Noun-Noun compounds". In Ray Jackendoff (ed.), *Meaning and the Lexicon: The Parallel Architecture, 1975–2010*. Oxford: Oxford University Press, 413–51.

Koptjevskaja-Tamm, Maria. 2013. "A Mozart Sonata and the Palme Murder: The structure and uses of Proper-Name compounds in Swedish". In Kersti Börjars, David Denison and Alan K. Scott (eds.), *Morphosyntactic Categories and the Expression of Possession*. Amsterdam: John Benjamins, 253–90.

Lakoff, George. 1987. *Women, Fire and Dangerous Things. What Categories Reveal about the Mind*. Chicago: The University of Chicago Press.

Lopriore, Lucilla and Cristiano Furiassi. 2015. "The influence of English and French on the Italian language of fashion: Focus on false Anglicisms and false Gallicisms". In Gottlieb Henrik and Furiassi Cristiano (eds.), *2015. Pseudo-English: Studies on False Anglicisms in Europe*. Berlin: De Gruyter Mouton, 197–226.

Mattiello, Elisa. 2017. *Analogy in Word-formation: A Study of English Neologisms and Occasionalisms*. Berlin & Boston, MA: De Gruyter Mouton.

Payne, John and Rodney Huddleston. 2002. "Nouns and noun phrases". In Huddleston, Rodney and Geoffrey K. Pullum (eds.), *The Cambridge Grammar of the English Language*. Cambridge: Cambridge University Press.

Rissman, Rebecca. 2015. *A History of Fashion*. Minneapolis: Abdo Publishing.

Schlücker, Barbara. 2016. "Adjective-Noun compounding in Parallel Architecture". In Pius ten Hacken Pius (ed.), *The Semantics of Compounding*. Cambridge: Cambridge University Press, 178–91.

Sharifian, Farzad. 2017. *Cultural Linguistics*. Amsterdam/Philadelphia: John Benjamins.

Sylvester, Louise, Mark Chambers, and Gale R. Owen-Crocker (Eds.). 2014. *Medieval Dress and Textiles in Britain: A Multilingual Sourcebook*. Woodbridge: Boydell.

Thanhauser, Sofi. 2022. *Worn. A People's History of Clothing*. New York: Pantheon Books.

Thompson Ford, Richard. 2022. Dress Codes: How the Laws of Fashion Made History. Ney York: Simon & Schuster.

Tiramani, Jenny, Maria Hayward, and Ulinka Rublack (Eds.). 2021. *The First Book of Fashion. The Book of Clothes of Matthaeus and Veit Konrad Schwarz of Augsburg*. London-New York: Bloomsbury Academic.

van Langendonck, Willy. 2007. *Theory and Typology of Proper Names*. Berlin: De Gruyter.

van Langendonck, Willy and Mark van de Velde. 2016. "Names and grammar". In Carole Hough (ed.), *Oxford Handbook of Names and Naming*. Oxford: Oxford University Press, 17–38.

Wickens, Mark. 1992. *Grammatical Number in English Nouns: An Empirical and Theoretical Account*. Amsterdam: Benjamins.

Wierzbicka, Anna. 1988. *The Semantics of Grammar*. Amsterdam: Benjamins.

Wotherspoon, Irené A. W. 1969. "A notional classification of two parts of English lexis". Unpubl. MLitt. Thesis, University of Glasgow.

Louise Sylvester

The Lexicalization of the Idea of Fashion in Later Medieval Britain

1. Introduction

The fashion of the medieval past is not easily legible through the representations that remain to us. The traditional view that the beginnings of fashion can be dated to the fourteenth century (Post 1955; Hollander 1994; Blanc 1997; 2002) has been countered by Heller, who argues that this claim is generally made by scholars whose focus is on the visual evidence of costume history (2007: 10). These are, perhaps, the researchers whose opinions we might expect to turn to for evidence of earlier fashion. Heller suggests, however, that this evidence, which mainly consists of cathedral sculptures, funeral bronzes, and a few miniatures, reveals only static images of what people were wearing and these do not us tell us what the clothes would have signified had they been worn by living people. Building on Barthes' (1967) conceptualization of a *système de la mode* (fashion system), Heller proposes that there was 'a period in the early to central Middle Ages in Europe when a fashion system did not exist, followed by a period in which one begins to appear' (2007: 19). She offers criteria for determining the presence of a fashion system within a culture (2007: 7–10). Those most relevant to this study are (in abbreviated form): (1) Fashion systems follow a theatrical logic of excess and exaggeration; (2) Words constitute the economy that gives and denies fashionable value to forms; (3) In a fashion system, criticism is constantly aroused by the rejection of the past and the tendency for continual change; (4) Because a major goal in a fashion system is consumption at the greatest possible level, when such a system is established there is a gradual movement towards equalization of appearances and accessibility to all social groups. In this chapter, the focus is most particularly on Heller's criterion (2), with some consideration of the others mentioned here. The terms relating to particular subcategories of clothing that were the focus of writing about (most usually against) fashion in the medieval period are examined from both an onomasiological and a semasiological point of view. Analysis of the resulting data in two case studies allows us to focus on elements of dress that were especially susceptible to changes in fashion.

2. The role of language in the conceptualization of fashion in the medieval period

It has been suggested that to see clothing through the lens of fashion, we need to access the desires (and other motivations) for the production and display of particular clothes and ways of wearing them. To achieve this, we need to pay attention to the language used to describe and discuss clothing (Heller 2007; Sylvester 2017). Barthes sets out the connection between fashion and language in his observation that fashion in clothing lies somewhere between the garments themselves and the words used about them. He observes that the fashion system is not actually about clothes or language, but 'en quelque sorte sur la "traduction" de l'un dans l'autre, pour autant que le premier soit déjà un système de signes' (1967: 8) ('the "translation," so to speak, of the one into the other insofar as the former is already a system of signs') (1983: x). Barthes concludes that 'ce n'est pas l'objet, c'est le nom qui fait desirer; ce n'est pas le rêve, c'est le sens qui fait vendre' ('it is not the object but the name that creates desire; it is not the dream, but the meaning that sells') (1967: 10; 1983: xii).

Discourses about dress in the medieval period are constructed in and by a range of text types: administrative, legal and literary (see Sylvester et al 2014). In wills by both women and men we see clothes represented as valuable items to be bestowed upon close relatives, beloved friends, servants, or religious foundations. Examples are provided by the wills of Isabel Gregory (1431–2): 'I be-quethe to Ione my dowter, a blew goune and a grene kyrtyll' (I bequeath to my daughter Joan, a blue gown and a green kirtle); Sir Roger Salwayn (1420): 'Also I will þat þe forsaid freres [the grey friars of York] haue all my gownes off cloth off

gold and off sylke, with-outyn þe ffurres' (Also I wish the above mentioned friars [the grey friars of York] to have all my gowns of cloth-of-
gold and of silk, but not the furs); and Roger Flore (1424–5): 'Also I wul
þat my gownes for my body, þe which ben ffurred whith pelure, be dalt
amongis my childre, to ilke after here degre and age, so þat Thomas
and Anneys haue four' of þe best. And I wul þat þe remenaunt of my
cloþes for my body be dalt amonges my seruauntes' (Also I wish my
gowns that I wear which are furred to be shared among my children, to
each according to their rank and age, so that Thomas and Anneys have
four of the best. And I wish the remainder of the clothes that I wear to
be shared among my servants) (Sylvester et al 2014: 46–47; 42–43).
In this period, clothes also had value as visible signifiers of rank. The
sumptuary laws show us an attempt to stratify social classes via restrictions relating to their clothing. This endeavour reveals possible fears
about a lack of social control (Sponsler 1992) and/ or the importance of
clothing as a semiotic symbol of social class, but one which was available to subversion (Sylvester 2017). The Act of October 1363, though
short-lived and possibly never enforced, offers a vivid example: grooms
are not allowed to wear cloth that costs more than 2 marks, or to wear
anything of gold or silver, or embroidered, enamelled or of silk, and
these constraints also applied to their wives and children. Esquires and
gentlemen below the estate of knight who do not have land or rent to
the amount of £100 a year may not wear cloth priced above 4½ marks
or cloth-of-gold, silk or silver, or embroidered clothing, and their wives
and children must wear clothing without any turning back or fur trim-
ming. Each rank is named in turn and similar restrictions imposed. The
problem is said to be the wearing of clothes that do not reflect the rank
of the wearer:

par cause qe diverses gentz de diverses condicions usent diverse apparaill nient
appertenant a lour estat; c'estassaver, garceons usent apparaill des gentz de mestire, et gentz de mestire apparaile des valletz, et valletz apparaile des esquiers, et
esquiers apparaill de chivalers, l'un et l'autre pellure qe seulment de reson apper-
tienent as seignurs et chivalers, femmes povres et autres apparaile des dames,
povres clercs pellure come le roi et autres seignurs'

(because various people of various conditions wear various apparel not appropriate to their estate; that is to say, grooms wear the apparel of craftsman, and
craftsmen wear the apparel of gentlemen, and gentlemen wear the apparel of

esquires, and esquires wear the apparel of knights, the one and the other wear fur
which only properly belongs to lords and knights, poor and other women wear
the dress of ladies, and poor clerks wear fur/clothing like those of the king and
other lords) (Sylvester et al 2014: 202–203).

2.1 Discourses of opposition

One of the characteristics of fashion, and a marker of the way that it is
constructed in the universe of linguistic conceptualization, is the discourse of opposition that it attracts. Lipovetsky takes the criticisms of
contemporary fashion as the marker of the moment in which a fashion
system was established in Europe:

> À coup sûr, depuis l'Antiquité, existe une tradition de dénigrement de futilité,
> des artifices et des fards: l'excès decorative est, dans ces temps, condamné, mais
> la norme d'ensemble du vêtement en usage est à l'abri des sarcasmes. Au con-
> traire, avec l'irruption de la mode, les pièces elles-mêmes du costume sont à
> l'origine de l'indignation; pour la première fois, le paraître ne repose pas sur un
> consensus social, il choque les habitudes et les préjugés, il se voit violemment
> condamné par les gens d'Église, il est jugé ridicule, incovenant, laid par les chro-
> niqueurs. La dernière vogue est sublime pour les élégants, scandaleuse pour les
> discordance des opinions iront désormais ensemble (1987: 43).

> (Without question, we can trace the tradition of denigrating frivolity, artifice and
> makeup back to ancient Greece and Rome; decorative excesses are condemned
> in periods governed by this tradition, but the prevailing overall standard of dress
> is exempt from sarcasm. With the emergence of fashion, on the contrary, specific
> components of dress are themselves targets of indignation. For the first time,
> personal appearance is no longer determined by social consensus; it affronts
> habits and prejudices, it is violently condemned by church leaders; it is judged
> ridiculous, inappropriate and hideous by contemporary chroniclers. The latest
> vogue is viewed as sublime by the elegant set, as scandalous by the moralists,
> and as ridiculous by the ordinary honest person; fashion and discordant opinion
> henceforth go hand in hand.) (Lipovetsky 1994: 28).

The reference to specific components of dress is borne out by the moral
and satirical works condemning contemporary fashion and the extracts
from medieval sumptuary laws collected in the reader *Medieval Dress
and Textiles* (Sylvester et al ed. 2014). Here we find prominent complaints concerning the male silhouette. These appear in the sumptuary
laws expressed in a restriction on the stuffing of doublets by yeoman

and any men of lower rank. This concern is echoed in poems, which also express disgust about the short cut of garments supposed to cover men's upper bodies. We also find long trains and long wide sleeves inveighed against in conduct manuals, a poem, and a petition requesting sumptuary legislation. Finally, the hacking about and altering of items of clothing is explicitly forbidden in conduct manuals.

3. Tracking change in the vocabulary of clothing

We can reverse engineer the diatribes against contemporary fashion in order to gain a sense of the elements of clothing that were objects of desire; that is, styles of dress that were understood to be fashionable. Turning to the vocabulary for the relevant garments and parts of garment, we can analyse the amount of lexis at the various levels of the semantic hierarchy, and investigate patterns of shift, obsolescence and replacement. We need to be aware that the later medieval period saw the borrowing into English of a large number of French terms (Schendl 2000; Durkin 2014; Trotter 2012). It has also been shown that contrary to the generally accepted account, the influx of loanwords did not lead to semantic shift or obsolescence of native senses and terms in this period; rather, most commonly, native terms and loanwords that were synonyms or co-hyponyms continued in use in the language alongside one another (Sylvester 2020; Sylvester, Tiddeman & Ingham forthcoming). In the semantic field of cloth and clothing, Piponnier and Mane point to 'the substitution of the vernacular for Latin and the use of terms with scant relationship to Latin, plus the borrowing of terms from one vernacular language to another' resulting in the growth of terminology responding to 'an outburst of creativity in styles of design, the advent of all sorts of new materials and the increasing significance of colour' from the thirteenth century onward, and especially in the fourteenth and fifteenth centuries (1997: 66).

The most useful place to look for the lexis of a particular semantic field is the *Historical Thesaurus* (*HT*). Here we find the whole of the vocabulary of English from the Old English period to the present day arranged within semantic fields. The classification is constructed as a semantic hierarchy. The terms are arrayed under three main categories, the External World, the Mental World, and the Social World, with the most general terms at the top of the semantic hierarchy. Each time a new component of meaning is added to the definition, we go down a level in the hierarchy, for example:

01.08.02 Clothing
01.08.02.01 Parts of clothing
01.08.02.01.01 covering specific parts of body
01.08.02.01.01.04 arm
01.08.02.01.01.04.01 parts of
01.08.02.01.01.04.01.01 cuff

The *HT* classification shows that, as expected, the superordinate level categories containing terms for 'clothing' and 'garments' in use in the later medieval period are large even though the category **01.08.02 n. Clothing** does not offer any terms with first dates of attestation after the Old English period and before 1300. There are 41 terms listed as being in use from 1300 until 1470. The subcategory immediately below this one, **01.08.02.01 garment/article of [clothing]** has 18 terms in use in the Middle English period. Most of the subcategories contain only four or fewer terms in Middle English.[1] The large number of terms relating to clothing suggest that the importance of this semantic domain in the later medieval period, as it appears to fulfil Wotherspoon's (1969) suggestion that if there is a high degree of semantic continuity in certain semantic fields, i.e. a concentration of a large number of minutely distinguished words and even of synonyms, a field may be a cultural theme.

---

1   In the category TRADE examined by Sylvester & Tiddeman (forthcoming), the largest categories are those at the highest level of the semantic hierarchy (Category Level 0). Of the categories at CL0, the largest, **Trade and finance** contains 13 nouns. There are two categories with 10 to 12 co-hyponyms, **Selling** and **Merchandise**; 10 categories have between five and nine co-hyponyms; and 20 categories have four or fewer, including four categories each containing only one term.

Further down the semantic hierarchy, as the terms become more specific in their senses, we find smaller subcategories. This data prompts a number of questions: how many sub-groups are found in each subcategory, that is, how fine-grained are the distinctions drawn in the names and descriptions of these items? How far are the terms contained in the subcategory polysemous? Do we see much obsolescence and replacement of vocabulary items? Two case studies are now offered examining vocabulary relating to items of clothing that were the objects of scorn and complaint (illustrated above). The vocabulary items that are discussed are at the more specialized levels, as it is in the particulars that we would expect to find the endlessly renewing novelty that fashion demands. As Heller observes, fashion systems offer 'choices between details rather than basic forms' (2007: 30). A particularly prominent example is provided by the dress of fashion-conscious young men ('galaunts'), a class of people whose clothes and appearance are a frequent topic in contemporary discourses about fashion. They are accused of changing their outfits very frequently, and, as we have seen, their clothes promoted a particular silhouette and were said to reveal too much of their bodies. Denny-Brown comments that they are seen to wear 'forms of clothing that stage their own stylistic mutability in the changing shapes of doublets, sleeves, hose, codpieces, and shoes or through their hybridized and pluralized colours, ornamentation, fabrics, and fillers' (2012: 149). We can begin by examining the vocabulary related to one of the most salient of their garments, the doublet.

3.1 Doublet

The database of the *Lexis of Cloth and Clothing project* (*LexP*) defines the doublet as a 'close fitting upper garment worn by men; frequently quilted, waist-length or hip-length, worn with or without sleeves, primarily from the fifteenth century onwards. Also a similar garment reinforced by mail and worn under armour (as pourpoint); a reinforced upper-body garment. Fourteenth-century references to the "doublet" and the "doublet of defense"/ "doublet of fence" usually refer to the reinforced or militaristic garment, while in the fifteenth century, the word could refer to either a militaristic garment or (more frequently) to the non-militaristic one'. Doublets were thus made of two layers of stuff with a layer of padding in between, made of cotton-wool or layers of discarded cotton or thick wool material, and had long hose attached to them by means of laces threaded through eyelet-holes. The doublet began as padded undergarment that knights wore underneath their hauberks. It shifted to being worn by itself as an outer garment, first by the highest social classes and later adopted by the middle and lower classes. The doublet became emblematic of the new fashions worn in this period, and has been seen by some scholars as the beginning of fashion as a concept (Newton 1980: 108; Hollander 1994; Denny-Brown 2012: 152). The *Oxford English Dictionary (OED)* editors note that the doublet 'had many changes of fashion, being at one time with, at another without, short skirts'. It has a further sense as a lining of a shield, and also a jewellery sense.[2]

The *HT* classification allows us to begin to assemble the set of terms representing doublets or doublet-like garments and to engage with questions about the meanings of the term *doublet*, and what other terms express similar meanings (to the central sense). We are able to examine this garment both semasiologically and onomasiologically to arrive at a sense of whether we can see fashion inscribed in this garment term and the categories and subcategories of vocabulary both above it (the more general, superordinate terms) and below it (the subcategories and sub-groups of co-hyponyms). The *HT* classification of the vocabulary in this domain places *doublet* in its own subcategory **13 doublet**. We can see how specialized this term is considered to be when we note that this sub-group is one of 25 sub-groups (most with further sub-groups hanging off them), below the subcategory **01.08.02.02.06 n.2 Clothing for body/trunk (and limbs)**, which is a subcategory of **01 garment/article of**, which is the first subcategory below the category **01.08.02 n. Clothing**. The place of *doublet* in the *HT* classification can be seen in Appendix A.

The *HT* subcategory **13 doublet** contains only one term from the medieval period, *doublet*, with the usage label 'obs. Exc. History'. Below it, is the subgroup **13.01 stiffening for** which contains the term

---

2   The jewellery sense is 'artificial or counterfeit jewel; this could be made of two pieces of coloured enamel, crystal, glass, or similar, cemented together; small ornaments for clothing in the Great Wardrobe'.

stenting, in use 1488–1658, a Scottish term meaning 'stiffening for a doublet'. These terms tell us something about doublets and how they were worn or how they changed over the period, refashioning the male silhouette, but not as much as we need to know. The related term *jack* in use in the 14th century is found under **14 jacket**,[3] but we have to go all the way down to **25 other**, containing other kinds of or parts of garments than those already categorized, to we find further terms which clothed the male torso in our period. The full list is as follows:

25 other
kirtle < cyrtel OE–
viteroke a1225
bleaunt c1314–a1400
surcoat a1330–
paltock 1350/70–1658
courtepy 1362–1483
tunicle 1377–1656
gipon c1386–1843 obs. exc. arch.
jupon c1400–1480 + 1826 obs. exc. History
petticoat c1425–2
wardecorps c1440–1483
coat-hardy a1450(3) obs. exc. History
placard 1483–

The precise meanings of these terms are somewhat elusive: they shift over time, and are sometimes attested with slightly different senses in French and Latin, both of which were in use in England in the later medieval period and garments originally worn by men accrue slightly different senses as they become part of women's dress (see, e.g. *kirtle* and *petticoat*). Several of the terms in this *HT* category do not appear to represent doublet-type garments. For *tunicle,* the *LexP* database gives a definition that suggests its use was confined to ecclesiastical use, with an extension to regal or ceremonial settings in Middle English, which

---

3   The *jack* appears to have the same origins as the doublet, being a jacket or tunic, stuffed and quilted worn over, or instead of, armour but it does not seem to have developed in the same way.

would be unlikely to attract anti-fashion opprobrium.[4] A *placard* seems
to be a panel or flap of clothing covering the chest or abdomen.[5] The
term *viteroke* does not appear in the *LexP*; the *OED* tells us that it is
'A ragged upper garment' and offers one citation from *Ancrene Riwle*,
suggesting that its usage is limited to women religious. The definition
of the *petticoat* in the *LexP* database suggests that the garment is a doublet, but only in the military version of that garment: it is a 'an arming
doublet, a padded jerkin worn under armour'. In non-military contexts,
it appears to form a possible part of an outfit that may also include a
doublet: it is a 'tight-fitting jacket or under-coat worn by a man, worn
over a doublet, shirt or similar; often padded; with or without sleeves'.
Having eliminated these items, we can attempt to discover whether the
others can be included within the set of 'doublet' terms using the definitions given in the *LexP* databse, which was compiled from definitions
given in an extensive set of historical dictionaries including the *OED*,
the *MED*, the *Anglo-Norman Dictionary (AND)*, and the *Dictionary of
Medieval Latin from British Sources (DMLBS)*.[6]

Kirtle: This term has two sense branches in the *LexP* database. Its first
sense is as a general term for an upper-body garment; a man or boy's
tunic, later a woman's gown. It was originally short, but the length
could vary. The term was sometimes used for a simple tunic with a
belt, and in the 14th century, it denoted a tunic (or a longer gown) worn
alone or under a surcoat, cote-hardie or gown. The term appears to
have been in widespread use in late medieval England: it is attested in
Old English, Middle English, Anglo-French, Latin, and Old Scots and

---

4   The *LexP* editors suggest that in its clothing sense, the tunicle was originally
     a 'small tunic', and was associated with various vestments. They note that the
     AND citations suggest only ecclesiastical usages, e.g. 'Chasubles, aubes e tuni-
     kes' from the 12th century. A further sense only attested in ME is regal or cere-
     monial garment, resembling the ecclesiastical tunicle; a richly ornamented robe.
5   The *LexP* editors definition is 'a panel of fabric, or a panel or flap of clothing;
     also, a fabric garment in the form of a panel covering the chest and abdomen,
     worn beneath an open gown, coat or jacket; a stomacher'. They note that while
     an 'armour' sense is attested in Anglo-Norman and Latin, in ME the term only
     refers to a garment.
6   For the full list of dictionaries used, see http://lexisproject.arts.manchester.
     ac.uk/dictionaries/index.html

occurs in a wide range of text types including wills, romances, sumptuary legislation, and petitions to Parliament. The kirtle is represented as a garment which may be made of russet and suitable for a servant to wear (in a will) or of rich cloth, e.g. sendal or ryche pall (in romances), but all these occurrences are quite late in our period and seem to refer exclusively to the woman's garment.[7] The term is difficult to pin down and may or may have a relationship to the doublet.

Bleaunt: The relevant definition in the *LexP* database, is a garment made of fine silk or similar material usually described as a tunic (the term can also represent a textile or a bedspread). The *LexP* database also draws attention to the fact that some 'French authorities describe the man's garment as a piece of military or ceremonial dress by the fourteenth century, often richly decorated and perhaps worn under, or in lieu of, the hauberk', which suggests a similar function to that of the doublet.

Surcoat: This term has one sense with four branches in the *LexP* database. None of them correspond precisely to 'doublet', but parts of the definitions offer a sense of a garment with the same derivation as the doublet. The first sense is a 'long overgarment' that is 'often described as being worn by a knight over the hauberk or the armour in general', it also has the sense 'a garment worn under the armour'. As we have seen, the doublet began as a garment that worn under armour and shifted to being worn as an outer garment, initially by the higher social classes. There is thus considerable overlap in the descriptions of the two garments and the ways they were worn.

Paltock: The *LexP* database definition describes a short upper garment with sleeves, usually described as worn by a man and frequently as being made of rich fabric. Most pertinently, it was sometimes worn as, or under, armour (like a doublet) and the definition concludes that it is 'a sleeved doublet'. Inasmuch as we can pin down the meaning of *doublet*, the paltock appears to be a co-hyponym, and indeed a near-synonym of the term.

---

7   A 'russet kyrtell furred with lambe' is left to a maid in the will of Margaret Asshcombe, dated 1434; 'a kurtyll of ryche palle' and kirtles 'of purpyl sendell' appear in *Emaré* and *Sir Landevale* respectively. For a discussion of *kirtle* and its use in a range of text types see Sylvester (2018: 79–84).

Courtepy: This term looks as if it is a garment for the upper body, but perhaps not one that is akin to a doublet. The definition in the *LexP* tells that a courtepy is a 'short cloak, mantle, jacket; short mantle made of rough-haired skins; a tabard or similar'. The ME citations all depict impoverishment, but one of the citations from a Latin gloss suggest that the courtepy was equivalent to a paltock.[8] Note Newton's comment below, however, suggesting that this garment was almost identical to a doublet.

Gipon and *jupon*: The *HT* subcategory includes both *gipon* and *jupon*, presumably because they have separate entries in the *OED*: a 'tunic, frequently worn under the hauberk' in an entry first published 1899 and not yet fully updated with the most recently modified version published online December 2021 and a 'close-fitting tunic or doublet; esp. one worn by knights under the hauberk, sometimes of thick stuff and padded; later, a sleeveless surcoat worn outside the armour, of rich materials and emblazoned with arms' in an entry first published 1901, with the most recently modified version published online December 2020. The *LexP* database additionally tells us that in A-F and Old French texts the jupon (jupoun, jopon; Old French gippon), generally refers to 'a close-fitting tunic or doublet worn under the hauberk'. Thus the two would appear to be one term with alternative spellings.[9] The relationship to the doublet is clear in the French senses, and note Newton's suggestion (below) that the jupon is almost identical to a doublet.

Wardecorps: The *LexP* database offers the definition 'outer garment; in some instances, a cloak or mantle, in others, a gambeson or padded tunic (worn under the armour)'. Like the *courtepy*, this looks as if it fulfils the same function as the military doublet only, but the citations,

8   The ME citations include 'A Clerk ther was [...] Ful thredbare was his ouereste courtepy' from the *General Prologue* to the *Canterbury Tales* and 'She was clad ful porely Al in an old torn courtepy' from the *Romance of the Rose*. In Latin we find 'unam curtepiam cum bona furura' from an account and 'bombacilium, A. cowrteby; bombicinum, A. a jakke; bombacinum, A. secundum quosdam aketoun; bombecina, a acton; lombesina, a paltoke' from a gloss (ME citations from the *MED*; Latin ones from *DMLBS*).
9   The *LexP* database gives the following alternate forms for *jupon*: gipoun, jupoun, iupoun, ioupoun, gypoun, gepon, gypon, gepoun, gryphoun, jopown, japon, jepun, jappon, iopon, gabon, jepouns, iopons, iompons.

which are almost entirely in Latin texts, link the wardecorps with other garments that are equivalent to the doublet, e.g. the aketon (see below).

Cotehardie: this term does not look as if it is equivalent to a doublet: according to the *LexP* database, it is a 'form-fitting, sleeved, knee-length overgarment, with a long bodice joined to a full skirt often worn under the doublet or kirtle' said to have been popular in the fourteenth century, having evolved from the close-fitting surcoat. It seems that the French version of this garment was equivalent to a doublet, however (see Newton's definition quoted below).

We may add further terms to our onomasiological set. For example, a search of the *MED* suggests that we should include the term *cōte*.[10] We may also note that Newton suggests that 'it is doubtful whether at any one time the exact differences between an aketon, a pourpoint, a doublet, a courtpiece and a jupon were absolutely defined. In France the cotehardie comes into this category, and in England, from the early 1360s, the paltok' (1980: 134).

Aketon: The *LexP* definition is 'a quilted jacket, worn as padding underneath a breastplate, or worn alone, as a decorative garment worn on top of armour'. A note on the garment shows the connection to the doublet and other terms in the onomasiological set: 'The short garment described as an acton (aketon) is related in shape and cut to many other (primarily) male garments of the later medieval period, and is occasionally used interchangeably with them - including the pourpoint, the doublet, the courtepy, the jupon and the English paltok'.

Pourpoint: The *LexP* definition describes this garment as a 'doublet (often stuffed or quilted)', noting that it was originally soft armour (12th to 14th centuries), worn under metal armour and adding that the pourpoint became particularly popular in the 15th century as male civil costume. The term appears to be synonymous with *doublet*.

Cote: The *LexP* definition suggests that this is a 'covering or outer garment fitted to the upper body, extending below the hip, open at the front

---

10   To discover if there were terms listed in *MED* not present in the *HT* (for which the source is the *OED*), 'reverse look-ups' were carried out. This was the methodology used to populate the domains in the *BTh* and involves making use of the definition search function in the *MED*.

or side, generally sleeved that took many forms throughout the medieval period, including the coat-armour, embroidered or painted with armorial bearings and often worn over the armour. The *MED* definition invokes several garments which appear in the onomasiological set of doublet-related terms: 'A tunic or kirtle (worn by men or women, either alone or under a mantle or other overgarment); also, a kind of surcoat or cote-hardie'.

The onomasiological set of terms equivalent to *doublet* suggest that this was a salient element of dress for men. The number of co-hyponyms and near-synonyms with overlapping senses suggest that we would not be wrong to associate this item with notions of desire and fashion in the later medieval period. The definitions alone cannot confirm this idea, but the complaints and anti-fashion diatribes in which it features offer supporting evidence. As noted above, doublets are the subject of exhortations and complaints and occasionally these reflect the concerns we have seen about preserving the distinctions in dress between the different social classes. Upper-body garments worn by men are a focus of concern about the male silhouette. This complaint is found in the late 14th-century poem complaint poem in Latin and English, titled by Robbins (1975: 1439) 'On the Times of Richard II' (in Fairholt's 1849 edition it is called 'A Satire on Manners and Costume', which is also the title of the extract in Sylvester et al. 2014). The narrator excoriates men of fashion thus: 'Brodder then ever God made humeris sunt arte tumentes;/ Narow thay bene, thay seme brod, nova sunt haec respice gentes/ Thei bere a new faccion, humeris in pectore tergo' (Broader than ever God made, they puff out their shoulders artificially;/ They are narrow, though they seem broad, these gents have the 'new look'/ They wear a new fashion, with the shoulder sat at the back of the chest) (Sylvester et al. 2014: 166–167). This complaint is echoed in the poem *Ballad against Excess in Apparel especially in the Clergy* composed in the mid-15th century, which mentions 'short stuffede dowblettes' (short stuffed doublets) (Sylvester et al 2014: 168–169). The poem is titled by Robbins 'Against Proud Galaunts' because of its first part which blames men of fashion – the second part offers the gallants' reply to these charges, namely that priests also follow the fashions in dress for short stuffed doublets and pleated gowns and are as lewd as the gallants they condemn (Robbins 1975: 1470). This complaint is echoed in the sumptuary laws of April 1463 where we find restrictions on the placing of 'eny bolsters nor stuffe of wolle, coton nor cadas, nor other stuffer in his doublet' (any padding or stuffing of wool, cotton or caddis, or any other material in his doublet) by yeoman and any men of lower rank (Sylvester et al 2014: 226–227).

The *HT* has a subcategory **14 padding** a subcategory of **01.08.02.01 n.2 Parts of clothing**. The subcategory contains no medieval terms, though there is a sub-group which hangs off this sub-category, **14.01 protuberance made by** which contains one lexical item, boss c1380. As we have seen, however, padding was an element of dress in the later medieval period which partly shaped the silhouette and which was much complained about. The *MED* offers '1. (c) that with which something is filled or stuffed: the padding of a dou-blet' with the helpful citation 'a1500(1465) Leversedge Vision (Add 34193)29: Orden the a playn dowblette with [out] stuffing and bol-sters (*MED* s.v. *stuffing* ger.). Even this element appears to have been subject to fashion. Newton points out that the characteristic padding over the belly seen in the 1350s quickly gave way to a different shape created by the belt being low and the tunic moulded to the natural waist which was made to look narrower by adding padding round the chest. This was increased over the 1360s until the chest looked almost spherical (1980: 54).

Further complaints about male dress focus on the cut of the upper-body garments. The author of the fourteenth-century poem, *A Dispiti-son Bitwene a God Man and Þe Devel* complains that: 'Muche meschef and gret colde: On his hers he has,/ Men miȝte, ȝif he brech weore to-tore: Seon his genitras' (He has much suffering and great cold on his arse: men could see his genitals, if he were to tear his underwear) (Sylvester et al 2014: 164–165). In his *Instructions to his Son*, Peter Idley comments on the same men's garments: 'They be cutted on the buttok even aboue the rompe./ [. . .] And if they shull croke, knele, othir crompe,/ To the middes of the backe the gowne woll not reche:/ Wolde Ihesu they were than without hoose or breche!'
(they are cut on the buttocks even above the rump. [. . .] and if they should bend, kneel, or crouch, the gown will not reach to the middle of the back: God's will, they would then be without hose or breeches) (Sylvester et al 2014: 186–187).

3.2 Sleeves

As noted above, sleeves were a subject that attracted opprobrium in medieval diatribes against fashion. They are found in two different categories of the *HT*:

> **01.08.02 Clothing**
> **01.08.02.02.07 Clothing for arms n.**
>
> **01 sleeve**
> sleeve < sliefe OE–
>
> **01.08.02.01 n.2 Parts of clothing**
> **01 covering specific parts of body**
> **01.04 arm**
> sleeve < sliefe OE–
> **01.04.01.02 other**
> foresleeve 1377–c1523
>
> **01.04.02 types of**
> manche/maunche 1391–1688
> poke 1402–1432/50

These entries do not give us a great number of terms, though we should also bear in mind that variation was achieved by the presence or absence of sleeves. In his discussion of surcoats, Chambers notes that the French bookkeeper of the Angevin *documents en français* of 1278–1280 includes both open and closed surcoats, 'and he distinguishes them only by noting the presence or absence of *manches* (sleeves)'. Chambers goes on to observe that in the same accounts 'from the end of the 1270s, both noblewomen and lawyers are described as owning a 'seurcot ouvert' with sleeves, implying that a sleeveless version would have been standard' (2011: 95). Lacking a wide range of lexical items denoting 'sleeve', we can focus on terms which suggest variety in the style of sleeves:

Manche/maunche: The *LexP* database gives the sense 'a sleeve; cuff'.
Poke: The principal sense seems to be a bag or pouch or sack. The *LexP* database has a second sense, based on the first, suggesting that the meaning is a bag shape or puffed-out protuberance in a cloth garment but that this refers to 'the bag-shaped, "bagpipe" or bombard sleeve, occasionally referred to as a "poky sleeve", with the opening

sewn up to the wrist, like a bag, which could in fact be used as a bag. The editors suggest that we are dealing with a fashion item, noting that 'this fashion became especially popular during Henry VI's reign (circa 1400 - post 1450)'.

This onomasiological approach can be augmented with lexical items that are listed in the *MED*:

> doublet sleves a.1474
> sleeves to be worn with a doublet;
>
> riven sleves, 1437
> ornamentally slit sleeves;
>
> round sleves 1437
> voluminous sleeves;
>
> trompe sleves 1437
> ?narrow tubular sleeves

These few items are enough to give us a picture of variety in the way that sleeves may have been worn. Voluminous sleeves feature in the diatribes against fashionable styles of clothing. They are mentioned in Robert of Brunne's *Handlyng Synne*, written in 1303. In Hoccleve's poem *The Regiment of Princes*, composed 1411–1412 he expresses his disgust at seeing them: 'But this me thynkith an abusioun,/ To see oon walke in gownes of scarlet/ Twelve yerdes wyde, with pendaunt sleeves doun/ On the ground' (But this I consider a violation of propriety to see someone walk in a gown of scarlet twelve yards wide with sleeves hanging down to the ground) (Sylvester et al 2014: 168–171).

The grounds for complaint are in some cases extravagance (the amount of fabric such a fashion demands means that one who affects this style will not have enough money to feed his household). The complaints about long, full sleeves sometimes go beyond the excess (of fabric, style, and pride) that this fashion demands, and point to concerns about gender roles; for instance, masculinity and the expectations associated with it. Hoccleve makes this point when he says:

> I putte cas that his foos him assaille
> Sodeynly in the street: what help shal he
> Whos sleeves encombrous so syde traille

Do to his lord? He may him nat availle;
In swich a cas he nis but a womman;
He may nat stande him in stide of a man.

(I put the case to you that his enemies suddenly attack him in the street: what
help would he be whose unwieldy sleeves hang down so as to be swept elegantly
along give to his lord? He cannot assist him. In such a case he is nothing but a
woman; he cannot stand in the place of a man.) (Sylvester et al 2014: 172–173).

Wide sleeves and trailing gowns are prohibited (to certain strata of
society); we may note a parliamentary petition of September 1402
(Henry IV), requesting sumptuary legislation: 'qe nulle homme, si ne
soit banret ou de pluis haute estate, use [...] grosses maunches pen-
dantz overtez ne closez' (that no man of lesser rank than a banneret
should use [...] large sleeves hanging open or closed) (Sylvester et al
2014: 208–209). The Act of the Scottish Parliament, March 1429 states
that 'allan*er*ly centynal ȝemen in lord*is* housis at rid*is* w*ith* gentill me*n*
þar mast*er*is þe quhilk*is* sal haf narow slewis & litil pok*is*& ry*t* sa þ*at*
þe com*mo*nis wif*is* [...] wer nouþ*er* lang tail na syde nekit hud*is* na
pok*is* on þar slef*is*' (only sentinel yeomen in lords' houses that ride with
gentlemen, their masters; [whose clothes] shall have narrow sleeves
and little pokes. And likewise neither that commoners' wives ... wear
either long tail, nor side necked hoods, nor pokes on their sleeves) (Sylvester et al 2014: 212–213).

    We note that one of the styles of sleeve that is lexicalised in the
Middle English period is *riven sleves*. This refers to the style of cutting
garments. Piponnier and Mane observe that 'hems and sleeves could be
scalloped or dagged in fancy shapes (such as leaves) [...]. The slashes
in the skirt and sleeves were lined in the same way; when the fashion
for tight cuffs returned, the slits were used as openings for the arms
so that the sleeves of the doublet could be displayed' (1997: 68–69).
Blanc comments that it remains essential for outer garments to reveal
the lower garment, noting that the trailing sleeves of the *surcots* reach
the ground, while also showing the clothing worn beneath, mentioning
also form-fitting sleeves that opened at the elbow to reveal the sleeve of
the garment underneath (2002: 162).

    This kind of cutting or dagging was not restricted to sleeves: it is
discussed in relation to other garments, and is a feature of expensive
bedclothes also, e.g. 'a keuerlit of selk ypoynet in that on side tawne,
and in that other side blu' (a slashed silk coverlet with one side tawny

and the other blue) is bequeathed by Lady Alice West to her daughter (Sylvester et al 2014: 32–33).

10 opening/slit
slit a1250–
spare a1300–c1700
vent 1459–1587 + 1828–

Slit: The *LexP* database notes that the verb is part of the manufacture of clothes: 'to split or cut open; in textile uses, refers to the cutting of an opening in a fabric or garment. Also as the past participle'. It also has a 'decoration' sense: 'a tear or slit in a garment'.

Spare: The first definition in the *LexP* database is 'an opening or slit in a garment; sometimes for decorative purposes, but also into which hands or objects might be placed'. Further senses relate to belts and buckles, and a late-15th century meaning 'a long sleeve' (translating Latin *manubium*).

Vent: slit or opening (in a garment). The *LexP* database adds: 'In some uses, extending the vertical length of the garment, trimmed with fur or fine cloth, and/or fastened closed'.

We can augment this set of terms with lexical items drawn from the *MED*:

Dēslatered ppl.?a1425(a1400) The *LexP* database suggests that this term is used for 'describing a garment that has been cut or slashed for ornamentation'.

Tagged adj. c.1425 'of a garment: cut in such a way as to have a loose hanging portion of fabric, slit so as to hang in points, slashed'. The *LexP* database also offers *tag*: 'with regard to cloth and clothing: the flap of a slashed garment', which is slightly different from the *MED* definition, which does not include the idea of a 'slashed garment'.

Cutted ppl. a.1300-c1600 This term is not included in the *LexP* database. The *MED* definition is 'ornamented with slashes'.

Cut-werk n. 1543(1464) The *LexP* database offers the definition 'decorative slashes or ornament; specifically a style of ornamentation caused by cutting the cloth of a garment so that the lining or undergarment is visible'.

There are, then, quite a number of terms for slashing or slitting garments, and unlike their modern equivalents, their meanings are specific: all the definitions mention garments and most ornamentation. The idea that we may be dealing with a fashion in garments, suggested by the clothing historians, is borne out by its presence in the conduct literature of the later medieval period. Hacking about and altering of items of clothing is explicitly forbidden in conduct manuals *Handlyng Synne*, Robert Brunne orders, 'Ne dysgyse nat þy cloþyng' (Do not fashion your clothing in a new-fangled way) (Sylvester et al 2014: 146–147). In his *Instructions to his Son*, Peter Idley orders him to 'Leve cuttyng and Iaggyng of clothis' (Refrain from cutting and slashing your clothes) (Sylvester et al 2014: 182–183). We also find this custom lampooned in the poem 'A Satire on Manners and Costume': 'Now knokelyd elbowes manace laqueant lacerale;/ In frost and snowes, ut aves spectant laqueatæ' (Their slit sleeves expose their knobby elbows/ They look like snared birds in frost and snow) (Sylvester et al. 2014: 166–167)

4. Conclusion

It is both tempting and difficult to decipher traces of fashion in the medieval period. It seems as if the images that remain to us are not really helpful: they cannot speak to us about the attitudes to their clothing of their wearers even when they are images of real people who lived and spoke. In his description of an encounter with a pair of medieval shoes in the Museum of London, Kelly observes that 'in order to distinguish between things – in order to recognise a function and meaning for things beyond what their initial plasticity dictates – humans need words' (2010: 57), finally concluding that 'we can only access the means by which things are accommodated into past conceptualisations of social life. The things themselves remain mute' (2010: 70). For the medieval period, we mostly lack even things. What we do have, however, are the conceptualisations. In this paper, I have tried to bring two pieces of evidence together. First, the vocabulary items that express garments and parts of garments at the lowest and most precise level of the semantic hierarchy, in the hope of catching a glimpse of movement and shift in the lexis, signs of the multiplying of terms that suggest the kinds of minute changes that signify fashion. The evidence from the *HT* and the *MED* showed where we can trace a multiplicity of terms with almost indistinguishable differences in meaning, in some cases actually indistinguishable now, but perhaps not for their original speakers.

I was able to locate particular ways of wearing the items of clothing: sleeves voluminous or narrow (or both in the same garment); the slashing or cutting of hems or sleeves or whole garments. These styles were suggestive of the kinds of desire that drive fashion, in particular the desire for novelty, 'a new faccion'. The other key piece of evidence was the discourses around clothing and how it was worn, and in particular the discourses of opposition that have been noted as signifiers of fashion. These are rife in the medieval period, across a range of text types. Building on the idea that fashion is constructed in language, and combining approaches from historical lexicography and discourse, I hope that this paper has cast some light on fashion in late medieval England.

Appendix

The categories and subcategories within which *doublet* is located in the *HT* classification:

01.08.02 Clothing

- 01.08.02.01 Parts of clothing
- **01.08.02.02 Types/styles of clothing**
- 01.08.02.03 Wearing clothing
- 01.08.02.04 Providing with/covering with clothing
- 01.08.02.05 Tailoring/making clothes

- **01.08.02.02 Types/styles of clothing**

  - 01.08.02.02.01 Underwear
  - 01.08.02.02.02 Outerwear
  - 01.08.02.02.03 Headwear

- 01.08.02.02.04 Neck-wear
- 01.08.02.02.05 Clothing for head or neck or body
- **01.08.02.02.06 Clothing for body/trunk (and limbs)**
- 01.08.02.02.07 Clothing for arms
- 01.08.02.02.08 Clothing for hands
- 01.08.02.02.09 Clothing for legs
- 01.08.02.02.10 Footwear
- 01.08.02.02.11 Clothing for head and body
- 01.08.02.02.12 Set/suit of clothes
- 01.08.02.02.13 One-piece garment
- 01.08.02.02.14 Bag/pouch worn on person
- 01.08.02.02.15 Umbrella/protection against bad weather
- 01.08.02.02.16 Parasol/protection against sun
- 01.08.02.02.17 Stick/cane

- **01.08.02.02.06 Clothing for body/trunk (and limbs)**

  01   clothing for shoulders
  02   clothing for chest/breast
  03   bodice
  04   shirt
  05   T-shirt
  06   worn beneath woman's gown
  07   sleeveless sports garment
  08   for exercise
  09   for jockey
  10   jumper/jersey
  11   cardigan
  12   waistcoat
  13   **doublet**
  14   jacket
  15   jerkin
  16   coat
  17   heraldic coat/vest
  18   dress/robe/gown
  19   sari

20   that covers/protects other clothing
21   loose clothing
22   belt/sash
23   clothing for lower body
24   clothing for body and limbs
25   other

References

AND = Rothwell, William et al. (eds.). 1977–1992. *Anglo- Norman Dictionary*. London: MHRA. http:// www.anglo- norman.net [accessed 22 Feb. 2022].

Barthes, Roland. 1967. *Système de la mode*. Paris: Seuil.

Barthes, Roland. 1983. *The Fashion System,* trans. Matthew Ward and Richard Howard. Berkeley: University of California Press.

Blanc, Odile. 1997. *Parades et parures: L'invention du corps de mode à la fin du moyen âge*, Paris: Gallimard.

Blanc, Odile. 2002. "From battlefield to court: The invention of fashion in the fourteenth century". In Koslin, Désirée and Janet E Snyder (eds.), *Encountering Medieval Textiles and Dress: Objects, Texts, Images*. Basingstoke: Palgrave Macmillan, 157–172.

Chambers, Mark. 2011. 'Hys surcote was ouert': The 'open surcoat' in late medieval British texts. *Medieval Clothing and Textiles* 7: 87–109.

Denny-Brown, Andrea. 2012. *Fashioning Change: The Trope of Clothing in High- and Late-Medieval England*. Ohio: Ohio State University Press.

DMLBS = Dictionary of Medieval Latin from British Sources. 1975. R. E. Latham, David Howlett, and Richard A. Ashdowne (eds.), *Dictionary of Medieval Latin from British Sources*. London: Oxford University Press for the British Academy.

Durkin, Philip. 2014. *Borrowed Words*. Oxford: Oxford University Press.

Heller, Sarah-Grace. 2007. *Fashion in Medieval France*. Cambridge: D S Brewer.

Historical Thesaurus, version 4.21. 2017. Glasgow: University of Glasgow. http://historicalthesaurus.arts.gla.ac.uk/ [accessed 22 Feb. 2022].

Hollander, Anne. 1994. *Sex and Suits: The Evolution of Modern Dress.* Brinkworth: Claridge.

Kelly, Stephen. 2010. "In the sight of an old pair of shoes". In Hamling, Tara, Catherine Richardson (eds.), *Everyday Objects: Medieval and Early Modern Material Culture.* Farnham: Ashgate, 57–70.

LexP = Lexis of Cloth and Clothing Project database. 2012. http://lexi ssearch.arts.manchester.ac.uk/ [accessed 23 Feb. 2022].

Lipovetsky, Gilles. 1987. *L'empire de l'éphémère: la mode et son destin dans les sociétés modernes.* Paris: Gallimard.

Lipovetsky, Gilles. 1994. *The Empire of Fashion: Dressing Modern Democracy*, trans. Catherine Porter. Princeton and Oxford: Princeton University Press.

MED =Middle English Dictionary. 2018. https://quod.lib.umich.edu/m/med/ [accessed 22 Feb. 2022].

Newton, Stella Mary. 1980. *Fashion in the Age of the Black Prince.* Woodbridge: Boydell Press.

OED =Oxford English Dictionary, 2nd/ 3rd edn. 1989. www.oed.com [accessed 23 Feb. 2022].

Piponnier, Françoise and Perrine Mane. 1997. *Dress in the Middle Ages.* New Haven: Yale University Press.

Post, Paul. 1955. «La naissance du costume masculine modern au XIVe siècle ». *Actes du Ier congrès international d'histoire du costume, Venise, 31 août-7 septembre 1952.* Venice: Centro internazionale delle arti e del costume, 28–41

Robbins, Rossell Hope. 1975. *XIII. Poems Dealing with Contemporary Conditions.* A Manual of the Writings in Middle English 1050–1500, vol. 5. New Haven: The Connecticut Academy of Arts and Sciences.

Schendl, Herbert. 2000. "Linguistic aspects of code-switching in medieval English texts". In Trotter, David (ed.), *Multilingualism in Later Medieval Britain.* Cambridge: D. S. Brewer, 77–92.

Sponsler, Claire. 1992. Narrating the social order: Medieval clothing laws. *Clio* 21: 265–283.

Sylvester, Louise. 2017. "Dress, fashion and anti-fashion in the medieval imagination". In Bintley, Michael, Martin Locker, Victoria Symons, and Mary Wellesley (eds.), *Stasis in the Medieval West? Questioning Change and Continuity*. New York: Palgrave Macmillan, 253–270.

Sylvester, Louise. 2018. "A semantic field and text-type approach to late-medieval multilingualism". In Pahta, Päivi, Janne Skaffari, and Laura Wright (eds.), *Multilingual Practices in Language History: English and Beyond*. Berlin: de Gruyter Mouton, 77–96.

Sylvester, Louise. 2020. "The role of multilingualism in the emergence of a technical register in the Middle English period". In Wright, Laura (ed.), *The Multilingual Origins of Standard English*. Berlin: De Gruyter, 365–379.

Sylvester, Louise, Mark Chambers, and Gale R. Owen-Crocker (Eds.). 2014. *Medieval Dress and Textiles in Britain: A Multilingual Sourcebook*. Woodbridge: Boydell.

Sylvester, Louise, Megan Tiddeman, and Richard Ingham. Forthcoming. Lexical borrowing in the Middle English period: A multi-domain analysis of semantic outcomes. *English Language and Linguistics* 26(2): 237–261.

Trotter, David. 2012. "Middle English in contact: Middle English creolization". In Bergs, Alexander and Laurel Brinton (eds.), *English Historical Linguistics*, vol. 2. Berlin: De Gruyter Mouton, 1781–93.

Wotherspoon, Irené A. W. 1969. "A notional classification of two parts of English lexis". Unpubl. MLitt. Thesis, University of Glasgow.

Silvia Cacchiani

Nominal Constructs in Fashion and Costume: Names and Nouns as Modifiers

1. Introduction

This paper concentrates on terms in the history of changing fashion and costume, paying attention to English Noun-Noun constructs and nominal constructs with proper Name modifiers.[1] Following Booij (2010), *constructs* are understood as empirically attested tokens of constructions, or constructional schemas with different degrees of abstractness within a hierarchical lexicon, which unify properties at the phonological, syntactic and lexico-pragmatic levels, and form the bottom level of a specific pattern or schema.

Our question is one about the semantics of the linking rule R. Considering our focus on Names vis-à-vis Nouns as modifiers in nominal constructs, we need to define and describe both categories. We therefore address the issue in Section 2, mainly drawing on van Langendonck's (2007; van Langendonck, van de Velde 2016) landmark publications on proper Names, proprio-appellative lemmas and appellative Nouns. As a second step, in Section 3 we turn to the semantics of the linking rule R in composite Noun-Noun structures. Our starting point will be Jackendoff's (2010) list of functions in Noun-Noun compounds. This shall provide the apparatus that we need to then concentrate on Names as modifiers in Section 4. As will be seen, the basic modifier function CLASSIFY will be expanded in order to account for shifts from the identifying and individualizing function of proper Names to functions such as EPITHET (Breban 2018) and TYPIFYING uses (Koptjevskaja-Tamm 2013), which are often grounded in the COMMEMORATIVE

---

[1]   Notice that we understand *construct* as a cover term for both compounds and phrases (cf. Radimský 2015). See Lieber and Štekauer (2009), Bauer (2017) for attempts at drawing a line between compounds and phrases.

function (Schlücker 2016) and based on metonymy. Though conceptual metonymy takes pride of place in this study, occasional reference will be also made to other key concepts in Cognitive Linguistics, most notably non-operational ICMs such as Image and Frames, and operational ICMs such as conceptual Metaphor (Radden, Kövecses 1999; Baicchi and Ruiz de Mendoza Ibáñez 2010).

The analysis that we carry out is strictly qualitative. Data (both terms and meaning descriptions) is manually collected from two main publications: Lydia Edwards' *How to Read a Dress: A Guide to Changing Fashion from the 16th to the 20th Century* (HRD), published in 2017, and the 2017 second edition of *The Dictionary of Fashion History* (DFH2), based on a Dictionary of English Costume 900–1900 by C.W. Cunnington, P.E. Cunnington and Charles Beard, and now completely revised, updated, and supplemented to present day by Valerie Cumming. Other sources comprise the *Dictionnaire International de la Mode* (DIM), directed by Bruno Remaury and Lydia Kamitsis (1994/2004), Fashionary International's (2021) *Fashionpedia. The Visual Dictionary of Fashion Design* (FAS), and publications by the Victoria & Albert Museum of Design: Claire Wilcox and V.D. Mendes' 2018 revised and expanded edition of *20th-Century Fashion in Detail* (CFD20), Lucy Johnston's (2018) reprint of *19th-Century Fashion in Detail* (CFD19), and Susan North's 2018 revised and expanded edition of *18th-Century Fashion in Detail* (CFD18). The *Oxford English Dictionary online*, 2nd and 3rd editions (OED) and the www are also used to collect fashion terms and gather encyclopaedic information.

2. Names and nouns

The main emphasis of this study lies into constructs with names as modifiers. Our first question, therefore is 'What's in a name?'. To address the issue, this section deals with Names as the prototypical (sensu Rosch 1978) identifying category, appellative Nouns, and the ability of names to undergo metonymization and appellativization.

2.1 Names

Names are nouns and noun phrases that "denote a unique entity at the level of established linguistic convention, to make it psychosocially salient within a given basic level category [pragmatics]". Names *individualize, identify* and *localize* meanings (van Langendonck 2007: 4, 131; my italics) – which is apparent with personal names, bynames or place names, all "construed as countable and nongeneric (i.e. non-recursive) NPs" (van Langendonck 2007: 186). Also, they "[do] not (or not any longer) determine [their] denotation [semantics]" (van Langendonck 2007: 4, 131).

According to van Langendonck (2007; van Langendonck, van de Velde 2016), names form a prototypical category, with members ranging from more prototypical to nonprototypical, all the way to names that undergo conversion into nouns and adjectives (e.g., color terms). Prototypicality, or 'namehood', is assigned based on occurrence in specific constructions.

Prototypical names are proper names with a *proprial lemma* in the onomasticon, they occur in (close) apposition constructions (van Langendonck 2007: 125–128), and do not take a determiner in that inherent definites (van Langendonck 2007: 154–158). The following categories are especially interesting for purposes of this study, in that used as modifiers in fashion terms or as fashion terms themselves:

- Personal names

  (1.i) *Alexandra* [Given name]; (1.ii) *Grace (Kelly)* [apposition: Given name + Family name]; (1.iii) *(Prince) Albert* [apposition: Title + Given name]

- Place names

  (2.i) *Aran*; (2.ii) *Ascot*; (2.iii) *Balaclava*; (2.iv) *Bikini*; (2.v) *Capri*

- Animal names

  (3.i) *bear*; (3.ii) *sheep*

Turning to *nonprototypical* names, we select for analysis:

- Trade and brand names

  (4.i) *Aquascutum*; (4.ii) *Birkenstock*; (4.iii) *Burberry*; (4.iv) *Dior*; (4.v) *Hermés*

- Letter and number names

(5.i) *A*; (5.ii) 2

Importantly, proper names presuppose the basic *categorical* meaning (sensu Rosch 1978) of their referent (i.e., intension, sense or type specification; van Langendonck 2007: 76–79) – e.g. 'female human' in *Alexandra* (1.i) and 'island' in *Aran* (2.i). Three more kinds of presuppositional meanings can be the *associative*, the *emotive* and the *grammatical*. On the usage level, associative meaning can be introduced either via the name bearer or the name form (*Benjy, Jackie O'*). Classic examples of associative and emotive meanings are names of singers, football stars and other celebs, which take on positive meanings and are assigned to new-borns. As is natural, emotive senses might attach via encyclopaedic knowledge to the specific name, e.g. charm, elegance, and other positive connotations for *Grace* (1.ii), if reminiscent of the late *Princess Grace of Monaco*. (See also example 1.ii.a below and Section 4 for more on this point.)

2.2 Nouns

Unlike names (i.e. proper names), *Nouns* (i.e. common nouns) serve an *appellative* function: they classify (refer to a set), affirm their own basic category, and are stored in the mental lexicon.

Unlike nouns, names presuppose their basic category. For instance, *Alexandra* (1.i) presupposes the basic category 'female human', while *Aran* (2.i) and *Capri* (2.v) presuppose the category 'island'. Yet, names take on different meanings when used as modifiers in fashion terms, as illustrated by examples (1.i.a), (2.i.a), (2.v.a.i) and (2.v.a.ii):

(1.i.a) **Alexandra jacket**

(F)

Period: 1863.

A day jacket without a centre back seam, the front with a small revers and a collar, the sleeves with epaulettes and cuffs.

Presumably named after Princess Alexandra of Denmark (1844–1925), who married the Prince of Wales in 1863; various "Alexandra" and "princess" styles were named after this elegant woman. (DHF2: Alexandra jacket)

(2.i.a) **Aran knitwear**

(F & M)

Period: 9th century onwards.

A distinctive style of knitting found in the Aran islands which used thick unbleached wool and incorporating raised motifs including bobbles, cables and twists. There are different traditions and patters to the East and West coasts of Scotland and Ireland. One tradition produced horizontal patterns, another produced vertical patterns. Originally produced as **sweaters** for fishermen, from the mid-20th century the motifs have been used on other informal garments, such as cardigans, coats, etc., and have been copied in different countries.

See Guernsey. (DFH2: ARAN KNITWEAR)

(2.v.a.i) **Capri pants**

(F)

Period: 1950s onwards.

Close-fitting trousers reaching to just above the ankle, not dissimilar to **leggings**, but usually of a sturdier fabric. An American style popularized by the film star Audrey Hepburn (1929–1993) in various films, such as *Roman Holiday* (1953) and *Funny Face* (1957). (DFH2: CAPRI PANTS)

(2.v.a.ii) **Capri Pants**

With legs cropped at mid-calf length, Capri pants are a favourite style worn in a warm weather. First introduced in 1948 by European fashion designer Sonja de Lennart, Capri pants were named after the Italian Isle of Capri, where they became highly sought after in the late 1950s to the early 60s. American actress Grace Kelly helped popularize the style as she was one of the first movie stars to wear them on the island. (FAS: APPAREL, PANTS)

2.3 Multiple denotations and appellativization

The examples in Section 2.2 suggest we put special emphasis on conceptual metonymy. Indeed, Names can undergo *appellativization* via conceptual *metonymy* and turn into Nouns. Consider the register trademark *Birkenstock* ® (4.ii), from the shoe factory founder *Adam Birkenstock* (FAMILY NAME FOR FIRM NAME). Thanks to the ever-increasing popularity of its timeless and practical styles over the years, family name and shoemaking firm have come to stand for the product itself (PRODUCER FOR PRODUCT/BRAND). Accordingly, one-strap sandals, two-strap sandals, tongue sandals and other classics with the distinctive contoured footbed are all styles and designs produced and sold as *Birkenstocks* (4.ii.a). The original footbed itself is called *Birkenstock* (PART FOR WHOLE). Copies of the same styles can only imitate the original sandals, but are also called *birkenstocks* in general language, and not easily distinguished from so-called *Birkenstock Originals/Birkenstock originals*. That is, *birkenstock* has come to classify practical sandals that come in specific styles and is now also used as an appellative Noun and umbrella term for such a category – pretty much like *BIC pens/bics* for ballpoint pens in general.

(4.ii.a) **Birkenstock sandals**

(F & M)

Period: 1967 onwards.

The name derives from a German firm of shoemakers who can trace their history back to the late 18th century. In the early 20th century a contoured arch was developed, the first to be placed into footwear. This was the origin of the Birkenstock sandal, known in Europe before being produced in the USA and marketed worldwide after 1967. In addition to sandals, there are shoes with the same distinctive arch support. (DFH2: BIRKENSTOCK SANDALS)

(4.ii.b) *Signature styles / Shop online at BIRKENSTOCK Footbed*

SIGNATURE STYLE

BIRKENSTOCK sandals and clogs boast a timeless and sleek design, premium materials and outstanding functionality.

What they all have in common: the original footbed

The original BIRKENSTOCK Footbed, found in all BIRKENSTOCK sandals and shoes, is made in Germany and delivers comfort all day long. (https://www.birkenstock.com/us/campaign/signatures/)

Burberry (4.iii) and *Aquascutum* (4.i) illustrate slightly different examples. Consider the matching encyclopaedic articles in DFH2:

(4.iii.a) **Burberry**

(F & M)

Period: 1856–1900.

A firm founded in England by Thomas Burberry (1835–1926), with a specific association with a proofed, cotton basic fabric called gabardine which was used for rainproof clothing. A London-based business was started in 1891 and the various garments produced were aimed at country and leisure pursuits.

Period: 1900 onwards.

Two trademarks were registered in 1902 and 1909, gabardine and *The Burberry*, respectively, the latter referring to the coats it manufactured. The military coats of the 1914–1918 war included the distinctive **trench coat**, a **classic style** much copied and worn in civilian life.

In the latter part of the 20th century the distinctive, checked lining was used for accessories including bags, hats and scarves, and the company enjoyed a revival with new fashion lines in the late 1990s. (DFH2: BURBERRY)

(4.i.a) **Aquascutum**

Period: 1850 onwards.

Along with **Burberry**, a name synonymous with rainwear since the 19th century. Originally an English tailoring firm funded in 1951 by John Emary and widely known after he introduced a waterproof garment in 1853; this London-based business became internationally celebrated during the 1914–1918 war when they provided waterproof **trench coats** for British officers to wear. An innovative approach with new fabrics, processes and styles has ensured that the firm has retained its reputation for chic but practical outwear while adding many other product ranges.

See Classic style. (DFH2: AQUASCUTUM)

Burberry is a *multidenotative* name (van Langendonck 2007). Via conceptual metonymies such as FAMILY NAME FOR PRODUCER NAME, PRODUCER NAME FOR FIRM NAME and PRODUCER FOR PRODUCT, *Burberry* has become synonymous with rainwear in general and trench coats in particular. It is a product and brand name, now used of a number of products by the same company. As regards associative and emotive meanings, the Burberry trench coat and Burberry's distinctive checked fabric epitomise British timeless elegance and rustic classic style. Additionally, one of the many copies on the market might be called 'a burberry', to affirm the basic category 'trench coat', and thus come to work as an appellative Noun via *appellativization* (van Langendonck 2007).

Unlike *Burberry*, Lat. *Aquascutum* describes a patented waterproof wool (En. 'watershield, Lit.'). Metonymies such as FABRIC/PART FOR PRODUCT and FABRIC FOR COMPANY NAME motivate the shift from patent name to product and company name, all the way to brand name, for a range of products and accessories produced over more than one century. Notice, however, that unlike *Aquascutum*, only *Burberry* has enjoyed a huge revival at the end of the 1990s, and is popular enough internationally to stand for the semantic category presupposed by its most iconic product (trench coats).

Place names can also take an attributive function in fashion terms, with modifier selection based on metonymies such as PLACE FOR PRODUCT MADE THERE, PLACE FOR PRODUCT USED THERE, or more simply, PLACE FOR STYLE/DESIGN. Such terms may go all the way to form reductions to the left, as in *Ascot* (2.ii.a.i) / *ascot, Balaclava* (2.iii.a) / *balaclava*, or the *bikini* bathing costume (2.iv.a).

(2.ii.a) **Ascot, *n.***

Used elliptically for a fashionable race-meeting held at Ascot Heath in June; frequently attributive, applied esp. to hats, dresses, etc., designed for or suitable for wearing in the Royal Enclosure at Ascot. *Ascot tie* (see quot. 1957); also, U.S., simply *Ascot*. (OED: ASCOT, n.)

(2.ii.a.i) **Ascot tie**

(M)

Period: 1876 onwards.

The plain form of this was similar to the Octagon tie. The "Puffed Ascot" was puffed out in the centre. Both versions, usually of patterned silk, were often self-tied but some were ready made-up. (DFH2: ASCOT)

(2.iii.a) **Balaclava**

(M)

Period: 1854 onwards.

A woollen cap which covered the head and neck leaving the face revealed; worn by military personnel and named after the Crimean village of Balaclava where the battle was fought in 1854. (DFH2: BALACLAVA)

(2.iv.a) **Bikini**

(F)

Period: 1946 onwards.

A two-piece bathing costume supposedly named after the Bikini Atoll in the Pacific Ocean. Although such bathing costumes had been worn earlier in the century (and by female Roman wrestlers much earlier), this version, designed by French engineer Louis Réard, was more abbreviated and set a trend for decreasing usage of fabric and maximum exposure of flesh. (DFH2: BIKINI)

The ability of Names to identify multiple referents, we have seen, is called *multiple multidenotativity/multidenotativity*. With brand and product names, it can also be observed in examples such (4.iii.b), where the linguistic context makes immediately clear that 'perfume' is the presupposed category:

(4.iii.b) you smell nice, are you you wearing burberry? (sic) [category: perfume]

No, . . . it's Gucci II. (sic) (www.memegenerator.com)

Here, *Burberry* could be replaced by any luxury perfume on the market, including *Aquascutum (of London)*.

Broadly, *multidenotativity* is a feature of family names that undergo shifts from Given or Family Names of (bespoke tailors and luxury) fashion designers to their companies and products (hence, via conceptual operations such as the PRODUCER FOR PRODUCT metonymy). Setting aside the obvious shifts from Family Name to Company Name, Product and Brand Names, it is interesting to see whether socio-cultural and encyclopaedic knowledge at different points in time can restrict category presuppositions for names of luxury products and brands. For instance, in the fashion industry *Hermès* (4.v) has been long known for its creations in fashion, leather goods, saddlery, watchmaking, perfumery and table decorations. But to the general public the brand might as well only associate with the *silk square* (Fr. 'le carré (d'Hermès)') (DIM: HERMÈS). And, we may want to add, at present it might resonate with posh teenagers because of its *twillies*.

Still staying with luxury and high life accessories, elegant women aged 30 plus associate the brand name *Hermès* with silk squares, twillies, and, if also affluent ladies, with the category 'bag'. Since the 80's Hermès has been producing the iconic *Birkin bag* (4.v.a), also called *Hermès Birkin* (4.v.b), or *the/a Birkin* (4.v.b). Here, the metonymy POSSESSOR FOR POSSESSED underlies the shift from person name (*Jane Birkin*) to product name (*Hermès Birkin*). The product name presupposes the non-basic category 'designer handbag with considerable investment value' (4.v.b, 4.v.c). *Birkin* is *multidenotative* in another sense too, in that it identifies individuals ('bags') showing unique features. Indeed, a Birkin is made on demand and customized by the producer; also, it can be 'dressed up' and personalised by the owner herself, e.g. adding bag inserts and using Hermès twillies to go with the handles, to make it ever more exclusive.

(4.v.a) **Birkin bag**

(F)

Period: 1980s onwards.

The British singer/actress Jane Birkin (b. 1946) inspired this large leather **bag** created for her by Hermes in 1984. Highly practical due to its size and highly desirable due to the limited numbers made annually. It acquired worldwide fame through the American series *Sex and the City* in the 1990s. Subsequently the naming of bags after performers and models became a useful publicity gimmick. [. . .] (DFH2: BIRKIN BAG)

(4.v.b) *Hermes Birkin*: I love this bag for special occasions. For my 13th wedding anniversary, I brought it out for lunch at Jaan by Kirk Westaway. [. . .] go to Hermes and try their NON COVETED items. In other words, even if you do eventually want *a Birkin/Kelly/Constance*, with the first visit, avoid going in with the goal of getting a highly coveted bag. Just visit the store and explore – see how you feel about their home and office products, shoes, belts, fine and costume jewellery, watches, etc. It is much easier to interact

with the brand if you can enjoy their things in general. (https://happyhighl
ife.com/hermes-how-to-get-a-birkin/)

A similar line of reasoning goes for *Hermès Kelly* and *Kelly bag* (1.ii.a), named after 'Princess Grace of Monaco (1929–1982), formerly Grace Kelly'.

(1.ii.a) **Kelly bag**

(F)

Period: 1930s onwards.

Hermès, the French firm established in 1837, produced a classic handbag inspired by saddle bags in 1935. A smaller version of this achieved worldwide publicity in 1956 when Princess Grace of Monaco (1929–1982), formerly Grace Kelly, appeared holding one on the cover of *Life* magazine. After that this style was always known by her maiden name and came in a wide range of leathers and colours. Named bags were unusual until the 1990s; for instance, Chanel's quilted shoulder bag with its leather and gilt chain was called 2.55 because it first appeared in February 1955. (DFH2: KELLY BAG)

Based on cultural-encyclopaedic information from DFH2, it is easy to understand *Kelly bag* (1.ii.a) as the institutionalised model analogue that gives rise to local analogy in *Birking bag* (4.v.a). Sets of analogues coined since the 1990s (DFH2: BIRKIN BAG) have triggered a repetitive pattern and brought about a gradual shift towards a schema (Booij 2010) for naming bags, with Female Family Name as modifier (4.vi: *Jakie O' bag*) or head (4.vi: *Gucci Jackie O'*).[2] Broadly, this is at odds with older naming trends in the domain, e.g. calling bags after first date of appearance (5.ii.a, which uses numbers as names; cf. numbers as nonprototypical names in example 5.ii), or events and people that are still linked to that very moment as part of what we may call the Bag Production ICM, which holds good for the *Hermès Constance*, also called *Constance* or *Constance bag* (5.ii.b).

---

2   Notice that Jaqueline Lee Kennedy Onassis, born Bouvier, a socialite who served as the First Lady of the United States of America next to her first husband US President John Fitzgerald Kennedy, came to be known internationally as *Jakie O'* after marrying her second husband, the Greek magnate *Aristotle Onassis*. This accounts for recourse to a nickname (as against family name) in *Jackie O' bag* and *Gucci Jackie O'*.

(5.ii.a) *2.55* [later known as *Chanel bag*; FAS: ACCESSORIES, BAGS]

Chanel's quilted shoulder bag with its leather and gilt chain was called *2.55* because it first appeared in February 1955. (repeated from 1.ii.a, DFH2: KELLY BAG; my emphasis)

(5.ii.b) *Constance bag/Constance/Hermès Constance*

The bag was first designed by Catherine Chaillet in 1959 and was given the name in honour of her fifth child, Constance, having delivered the baby the same day that the first Constance left the Hermes production store. With its leather shoulder strap allowing the bag to hang freely, it soon became the favourite of former First Lady of the United States, Jacqueline Kennedy who popularised the Constance amongst Hollywood's elite. (https://bagsofluxury.com/news/hist ory-hermes-constance-bag/)

3. The semantics of the linking rule R: Nominal constructs with Noun as modifier

Section 2 gave us a working definition of Names and Nouns, while also touching upon metonymization, appelativization and multidenotativity, and the role of socio-cultural and encyclopaedic knowledge for identifying the categories presupposed by the name and the style associated with fashion terms. With these observations in mind, we can move on to discuss a list of functions that can flesh out the semantics of the linking rule R in the naming and nominal constructs under scrutiny. To this purpose, we shall draw on work within Jackendoff's (2010) Parallel Architecture (2010). Key concepts comprise argument and modifier schemas, proper function, action modality, and co-composition. While we set aside the argument schema, we adapt Jackendoff's (2010) work on other basic modifier functions to our purposes. CLASSIFY is held to be a very general relation, which can be filled out by more specific functions. Discussion of nominal constructs with Name as modifier is postponed to Section 4 for clarity.

3.1 Similarity

As clothing is designed around the human body, the Human Body ICM is readily assumed to play a key part in coining fashion term.[3] Importantly, male and female bodies are shaped into a number of silhouettes and lines, via metaphorical schematic shapes from source domains like the alphabet (letter shapes in *A-*, *H-*, *I-* and *Y-line*, 6.i), architecture and building (e.g. in *column dress*, 6.ii, a synonym of *I-line*, 6.i), etc. (e.g. *sack dress*, 6.iii). Any associative meaning can only develop based on our encyclopaedic knowledge of the fashion industry. And, for the general public, this is more likely to take place around the time a given trend, design, style or fad is in the fashion. Thus, the general public today is not likely to see dresses like *A-line* dresses or silhouettes (6iv) – introduced by fashion designer Christian Dior (1905–1957) after WWII and part of the French 'New Look' fashion trend – as ultra-feminine garments. Or, to take an opposite achievement, we can wear a (variant of the) *sack dress* (6.iii) – one of Balenciaga's most prominent and imitated signature looks – just because it is practical. But, not because it was originally designed by Balenciaga, nor because it originally represented a highly experimental and radical innovation, clearly intended to liberate women from the hourglass shape (http://kvadratinterwoven.com/balenciagas-shocking-bodies).

(6.i)   *A-line (dress/silhouette); H-line (dress/silhouette); I-line (dress/silhouette); Y-line (dress/silhouette)*

(6.i.a) **A-line** [dress]

(F)

Period: 1955.

One of three lines (*H*, *A* and *Y*) introduced by French designer Christian Dior (1905–1957) between 1954 and 1955. The A-line was a reworking of the 1954 H-line and coats, dresses and suits with this cut formed a triangle from shoulder to

---

3   See, in this respect, fashion terms for items of apparel, details and accessories that are clearly built around human body parts, along the vertical or horizontal axis: *top* and *bottoms* (e.g. in a two-piece garment); *mini-, midi and maxidresses*; *handbags* and *shoulder bags*; the *halterneck, off-the shoulder* and *one-shoulder necklines; single-breasted* and *double-breasted openings; low-cut* and *high-cut waistlines*; etc.

hem, with the cross-bar of the A below the bust or on the waist or hips. (DFH2: A-LINE)

(6.ii)   *Column dress*
(6.iii) **Sack dress**

(F)

Period: 1960 onwards.

A loose, short dress, often shaped into a narrower hemline. Designed by the Spanish couturier Cristobàl Balenciaga (1895–1972), it was copied by other designers and makers. (DFH2: SACK DRESS)

For all constructs, the basic function is 'N_2 that is SIMILAR to an N_1', where N_1 denotes the shape, and an image metaphor is activated. This is a very common relation in fashion terms, for items of apparel (6 above, 7.i.a, 7.i.b), details (7.ii), and accessories (7.iii).

(7.i.a)   *bell bottoms*; *tube dress*; *tunic dress*; *fishtail skirt*
(7.i.b)   *bib dress*; *bubble dress*; *petal dress*
(7.ii)   *olive button*; *horseshoe collar*; *petal collar*; *wing cuff*; *funnel neckline*; *horseshoe neck/neckline*; *balloon sleeve*; *batwing sleeve*; *bell sleeve*; *crescent sleeve*; *elephant sleeve* [in the shape of an elephant ear]; *mushroom sleeve*
(7.iii.a) *box bag*; *bucket bag*; *cartwheel hat*; *mushroom hat*; *boa (scarf)*
(7.iii.b) *cateye (glasses)*

Notice that the modifiers in *bib dress*, *bubble dress* and *petal dress* (7.i.b) only denote the most distinctive parts of the dresses ('N_2 HAS a detail/PART' & 'a PART is SIMILAR to N_1'). This is also true of *cateye glasses* (7.iii.b), where *cateye* maps one visual image onto another one, and thus likens rims and lenses to the shape of the 'feline eyeline style' in cosmetics (FAS: EYELINE STYLES) and the shape of cats' eyes in nature. Still staying with image metaphors, *bell bottoms* also involves mapping the shape of a bell onto the shape of the bottom of a pair of trousers, with a PART FOR WHOLE metonymy. More to the point, if we do not see *bottoms* and *trousers* as synonyms – which would most definitely be the case with a two-piece garment – *bell bottoms* involves mapping the shape of the whole bell onto the whole leg and perspectivizing the most perceptually salient part of the leg, i.e. the bottom:

7.i.a.i **Bell bottoms**

(F & M)

Period: 1960s onwards.

Sailors traditionally wore trousers that flared out from knee to ankle but, in terms of fashion, this style appeared in the 1960s with an exaggeratedly tight fit on the upper leg and a wide bottom flare. (DFH2: BELL BOTTOMS)

3.2 Location, modalities, composition

A linking rule that involves LOCATION can be approached from different perspectives. Because we are primarily interested in Names and, to a minor extent, Nouns as modifiers, we set aside the very many constructs that instantiate [P-N] nominal schemas – for instance, with the linking rule 'N is over/under something', as in (8.i), or (8.ii) in which the compound is elaborated in quasi-syntactic ways, as in *off-the-shoulder (neckline)*.

At this point, we want to talk about the constructs in (9), which fill out the LOCATION function in different fashions. As can be seen, the compounds in (9.i) involve temporal location ('during N_1'), cocomposition between N_1 and N_2 and a proper or characteristic function of N_2 ('N_2 whose proper or characteristic function is to be used/worn at time N_1'). On our view, social occasions are a special case of location (9.i.b): the constructs here are complex terms for dresses to be worn at different times of the day, e.g. *morning dress, cocktail dress* and *evening dress* ('N_2 whose proper or characteristic function is to be used/ worn at time/occasion N_1'). Assuming a metonymical shift (LOCATION FOR ACTIVITY/OCCASION) for *court*, we can also group *court dress* and *court shoes* along with *cocktail dress* and other constructs in (9.i.b).

(8.i)   *overall, overcoat; underwear, underskirt*

(8.ii)   *off-the-shoulder (neckline)*

(9.i.a) *day dress* and *nightgown; daywear* and *nightwear*, including the now forgotten *night-cap*

(9.i.b) *morning dress, cocktail dress, evening dress; court dress* and *court shoes; wedding dress* and *wedding suit; tea jacket* and *dinner jacket*;

'Characteristic modality' or 'proper function' account for the compounds in (10), including the neologism *work-from-home outfit*:

(10) *ballet dress; baseball cap; shooting coat; cycling pants, cycling shorts; court shoe; deck boot; running shoe; smocking suit, swimsuit; leisurewear, officewear, skiwear; work-from-home outfit*

Other functions involve HAVE ('N_2 that N_1 has'), as in the compound families in (11), and COMPOSITION ('N_2 is composed of N_1'), as in (12):

(11) *sailor blouse, sailor collar, sailor hat, sailor pin, sailor suit, sailor pants; cowboy boot, cowboy hat, cowboy jacket, cowboy pants*
(12) *sheepskin (coat/jacket); bearskin (hat)*

Both *sheepskin* and *bearskin* are based upon a PART FOR WHOLE metonymy. Yet, whereas a *sheepskin* might come in different shapes, the *bearskin* is the tall, iconic hat, made of black fur and worn by the British soldiers parading outside Buckingham Palace at the Changing of the Guards ceremony. We can therefore readily assume a culture-specific Bearskin Hat ICM (Benczes 2006).

4. The semantics of the linking rule R: Nominal constructs with Name as modifier

So far, we have addressed the definition of Names and Nouns, cases in the grey area in between their identifying uses (for Names) and appellative function (for Nouns) as well as appellativization via metonymy (Section 2), and diverse basic functions that fill out the relation between head and modifier in [N-N] nominal constructs (Section 3). This leads us back finally to a more theoretically-grounded description of the semantics of nominal constructs with Name as modifier, and of the role of Names in fashion terms.

Although a basic ARGUMENT structure ('N_2 by $Name_1$', e.g. *Chanel bag*) or a general CLASSIFY function ('$Name_1$ classifies N_2')

might at first sight appear to fill out and specify the semantic relation in the constructs at hand, there is more than meets the eye. At multiple stages in the paper we have been talking about a COMMEMORATIVE relation, 'N_2 is named after Name$_1$'. Indeed, Schlücker (2016; based on Warren 1978 and Ortner, Müller-Bolhagen 1991) has argued for positing a COMMEMORATIVE relation as part of the semantic-conceptual structure of compounds like the set of analogues in (1.iii.a), with *(Prince) Albert* (1.iii) as modifier, for items of apparel, details and accessories. They were given the name of Prince Albert of Saxe Coburg Gotha (1819–1861) after 1840, when he became the consort of Queen Victoria (i.iii.b). In other words, Prince Albert served as a trendsetter and 'style icon' for a number of items of male clothing which only rarely outlasted the end of the Victorian Age.

(1.iii.a) *Albert boots (Period:* 1840-ca. 1870); *Albert collar (Period:* ca. 1850 to early 20th century); *Albert driving cape, sac (Period:* 1860 to early 20th century); *Albert jacket (Period:* ca. 1848); *Albert overcoat (Period:* 1877); *Albert riding coat (Period:* 1881); Albert slipper *(Period:* After 1840); *Albert top frock (Period:* ca. 1860–1900); *Albert watch chain (Period:* 1860 to 1900) (DFH2)

(1.iii.b) **Albert slipper**

(M)

Period: after 1840.

A slipper with an extended vamp in the form of a tongue covering the foot; named after Prince Albert of Saxe Coburg Gotha (1819–1861), consort of Queen Victoria. Many items of clothing were given his name after his marriage to Victoria in 1840. (DFH2: ALBERT SLIPPER)

Fashion icons and their styles change over time – on a par with styles, markets and the fashion industry itself – as a result of political, economic, socio-cultural and technological changes (HRD). Broadly, *Prince Albert* (1.iii.a, 1.iii.b) or *Princess Alexandra* (1.i, 1.i.a) epitomised elegance in the second half of the 19th century, and the rich elite tried to imitate their styles. *Coco Chanel* was a couturier and style icon of the 1920s and the brand is still known for femininity and elegance. *Audrey Hepburn* and *Grace Kelly* still embody the glamour of the 1950s, *Jaqueline Kennedy Onassis* the classic elegance and *Jane Birkin* the casual and sometimes subversive beauty of the 1960s.

Staying with classic styles, let us zoom in on the *Hermès Kelly/ Kelly/Kelly bag* (1.ii.a) and the *Gucci Jakie O'/Jakie O'/Jackie O' bag* (4.vi) again. Epitomizing involves suggesting the presence of signature attributes. This can be accounted for within the EPITHET approach developed by Breban (2018). EPITHET (referring to attributes; cf. Breban 2018) is the metonymically motivated function that shifts the composite expression towards TYPIFYING (Koptjevskaja-Tamm 2013). The EPITHET dimension of the construct modifier introduces similar complex descriptions in the specifications *Kelly/Kelly/Kelly bag* and *Gucci Jakie O'/Jakie O'/Jackie O' bag*. The many replicas on the market of the *Jakie O'* and the *Kelly* bear witness to their iconic value and influential role. Both appear to be classic must-haves, and fakes and imitations try to approximate this exquisite and exclusive subtype. The bags replicate a well-established fashion style category inspired to Grace Kelly and Jaqueline Kennedy's signature styles. The meaning of the personal Name, which is not only and not exclusively identifying, is key to this type of branding. Based on our knowledge of the world, we construct the late Grace Kelly with reference to her glamorous and fabled life as a Hollywood actress first and Princess of Monaco later. In like manner, Jackie Kennedy Onassis is celebrated as an icon of enduring style, allure, and charm. These properties are part of the real world and known to the decoder, but the description is more complex than the one that could be given by intersective adjectives. These names are EPITHETS that come with positive meanings from the fields Status, Romanticism and Sensuality, Wealth, Power and Independence (Cotticelli Kurras 2013). To put it with Koptjevskaja-Tamm (2013), they TYPIFY.

While it is not new that modifying nouns serve as cues for activating world knowledge that is compatible with the head and for activating a selection task that involves the reconstruction of complex descriptions in nominal compounds, it should be clear by now that personal Names as modifiers serve as a reference point for the metonymic process of domain reduction (Ruiz de Mendoza Ibañez 2010): in plain English, the name of the style icon stands for selected attributes that are conceptually compatible (CELEB FOR STYLE). Thus, the name can semantically enrich the noun with highly seductive properties.

Besides classic elegance, *Burberry* (4.ii.a) or *Aquascutum* (4.i.a) will associate with brand values such as accountability and practicality; *Birkenstock* (4.ii.a, 4.ii.b) with practicality and comfort.

But, what about place names as modifiers in *Aran knitwear/sweater* (2.i.a), *Ascot/Ascot tie* (2.ii.a), *Capri pants* (2.v.a.i, 2.v.a.ii), *Empire line* (13) or *Delphos dress* (14)?

Aran knitwear (2.i.a) is easily accounted for with an argument structure 'something knitted by Aran locals', which minimally involves the PLACE FOR MAKER metonymy, and its description requires encyclopaedic knowledge of distinctive yarn and patterns, and intended users (2.i.a). We can also identify a PLACE FOR STYLE metonymy. In *Ascot/Ascot tie* (2.ii.a) the semantic relation is 'N$_2$ whose proper/characteristic function is to be worn at Name$_1$', and the association with positive attributes in the fields of Status, Wealth and Elegance (Cotticelli-Kurras 2013) is grounded in the PLACE FOR STYLE metonymy and the Ascot Race ICM. Ascot is a brand name by itself.

Capri pants (2.v.a.i; 2.v.a.ii) is a slightly different case (see also Biscetti and Baicchi 2019). The pants are named after *Capri* and the meaning can be explained via co-composition, characteristic function, geographic location and time as a special type of location. More simply, we can assume a PLACE FOR STYLE metonymy. At the time the pants entered the market the island was a must-go for celebrities and socialites. Yet, over the years the construct has lost connection with the original metonymy and the Elegant Resort ICM.

To conclude, let us consider *empire line* (13) and *Delphos dress* (14):

(13) **Empire line**

(F)

Period: ca. 1800–1820

The term is usually applied to the high-waisted, narrow and sinuous dresses worn by fashionable women throughout Europe during this period, and associated with the period of Napoleon's rule in France as First Consul and Emperor. Later revivals in the 1890s and in the 20th century, and its regular appearance in films and on television, have given it a classic status. (DFH2: EMPIRE LINE)

Empire is a temporal location and has an attributive (EPITHET or TYPIFYING) function in this construct, with associations that have

come down to the present, first and foremost an idea of 'classical simplicity'. Simplicity and classical style are also a feature of the *Delphos
dress* (14), inspired by and named after a classical Greek statue, the
Charioteer of Delphi. Here, the conceptual metonymy PLACE FOR STYLE
enables fashion professionals and fashionistas to arrive at a complex
description of the dress. The function is therefore EPITHET or TYPI-
FYING, and not LOCATION.

(14) **Delphos dress, Delphos gown**

(F)

Period: 1000s onwards.

A style of dress created by the Spanish Artist and designer Mariano Fortuny
(1871–1949). It paid homage to the simplicity of **classical dress**, using a method
of pleating thin silk, which was patented in Paris in 1909, and weighting the
dress together with thin cords and glass beads. The silk was coloured with natural dyes. These dresses were worn by artists, musicians and performers as a form
of artistic or **aesthetic dress** and enjoyed a revival when they became desirable
acquisitions for collections in the 1970s and later. (DFH2: DELPHOS DRESS, DEL-
PHOS GOWN)

5. Conclusions

The purpose of this paper was to investigate English terms and, more
particularly, nominal constructs (Booij 2010) with Noun or Name as
modifiers, in the changing history of fashion and costume. Starting on
the assumption that proper Names and appellative Nouns form prototypical categories with fuzzy boundaries (van Langendonck 2007;
Van Langendonck and van de Velde 2016), we have provided a qualitative investigation of a representative selection of terms that were manually gathered from encyclopaedic dictionaries, visual dictionaries,
and landmark publications on the history of fashion. Interestingly, the
analysis has shown that conceptual metonymy is an important determinant of the shift from the identifying and individualizing function

of prototypical place and personal names to classifying uses as appellative nouns, also in reductions to simplexes (e.g. *Ascot tie/Ascot/ascot*). Additionally, considering the linking rule R in the composite structures under scrutiny, it seems reasonable to suggest that, firstly, the COMMEMORATIVE function (cf., e.g., Schlücker 2016) underlies CLASSIFY (Jackendoff 2010) in specifications of the Name-Noun schema, and, secondly, the shift to EPITHET (Breban 2018) and the TYPIFY function (Koptjevskaja-Tamm 2013) can be motivated metonymically whenever associative/emotive meanings and complex descriptions enter into the picture, as in *Hermès Kelly / Kelly bag / Kelly*. This allows for complex descriptions, which cannot boil down to individual attributive adjectives. Another question concerned the potential for certain constructs and iconic products to retain their ability to convey complex descriptions, which turns out to be a matter of extant cultural and encyclopaedic knowledge (knowledge of brand, brand products, and style icons).

References

Baicchi, Annalisa and Francisco José Ruiz de Mendoza Ibáñez. 2010. The cognitive grounding of illocutionary constructions within the theoretical perspective of the Lexical-Constructional Model. Special Issue on "Cognition and the Brain in Language and Linguistics". *Textus* 23: 87–112.

Bauer, Laurie. 2017. *Compounds and Compounding*. Cambridge University Press: Cambridge.

Benczes, Réka. 2006. *Creative Compounding in English. The Semantics of Metaphorical and Metonymical Noun-Noun Combinations*. Amsterdam: John Benjamins.

Biscetti, Stefania and Annalisa Baicchi. 2019. Space oddity: What fashion terms can reveal about the English and Italian cognitive systems. *Culture, Fashion and Society Notebook* 5: 3–28.

Booij, Geert E. 2010. *Construction Morphology*. Oxford: Oxford University Press.

Breban, Tine. 2018. Proper names used as modifiers: A comprehensive functional analysis. *English Language & Linguistics* 22(3): 381–401.

CFD18: North, Susan. 2018. *18th-Century Fashion in Detail,* 2nd rev. edn. London: Thames & Hudson, V&A.

CFD19: Johnson, Lucy. 2018. *19th-Century Fashion in Detail.* London: Thames & Hudson, V&A.

CFD20: Wilcox Claire and V. D. Mendes. 2018. *20th-Century Fashion in Detail,* 2nd rev. edn. London: Thames & Hudson, V&A.

Cotticelli Kurras, Paola. 2013. "Italian commercial names: Brand and product names on the globalised market". In Oliviu Felecan and Alina Bughesiu (eds.), *Onomastics in Contemporary Public Space.* Newcastle upon Tyne: Cambridge Scholars, 257–276.

DFH2: Cumming, Valerie. 2017. *The Dictionary of Fashion History, 2nd ed. Based on a Dictionary of English Costume 900–1900 by C.W. Cunnington, P.E. Cunnington and Charles Beard.* London: Bloomsbury.

DIM: Remaury, Bruno and Lydia Kamitsis. 1994/2004. *Dictionnaire International de la Mode.* Paris: Éditions du Regard.

FAS: Fashionary International. 2021. *Fashionpedia. The Visual Dictionary of Fashion Design.* Hong Kong: Fashionary International.

HRD: Edwards, Lydia. 2017. *How to Read a Dress: A Guide to Changing Fashion from the 15th to the 20th Century.* London: Bloomsbury

Jackendoff, Ray. 2010. "The ecology of English Noun-Noun compounds". In Ray Jackendoff (ed.), *Meaning and the Lexicon: The Parallel Architecture, 1975–2010.* Oxford Oxford University Press, 413–51.

Koptjevskaja-Tamm, Maria. 2013. "A Mozart Sonata and the Palme Murder: The structure and uses of Proper-Name compounds in Swedish". In Kersti Börjars, David Denison and Alan K. Scott (eds.), *Morphosyntactic Categories and the Expression of Possession.* Amsterdam: John Benjamins, 253–90.

Lieber, Rochelle and Pavol Štekauer Pavol. 2009. "Status and definition of compounding". In Rochelle Lieber and Pavol Štekauer (eds.), *The Oxford Handbook of Compounding.* Oxford: Oxford University Press, 3–18.

OED: *Oxford English Dictionary online*, 2nd and 3rd edn. (1989–2021). Available at <www.oed.com>

Ortner, Lorelies and Elgin Müller-Bolhagen. 1991. *Deutsche Wortbildung: Typen und Tendenzen in der Gegenwartssprache. Vierter Hauptteil: Substantivakomposita*. Berlin: Walter de Gruyter.

Radden, Günter and Zoltan Kövecses. 1999. "Towards a Theory of Metonymy". In Klaus-Uwe Panther and Günter Radden (eds.), *Metonymy in Language and Thought*. Amsterdam: John Benjamins, 17–59.

Radimský, Jan. 2015. *Noun+Noun Compounds in Italian. A Corpus-based Study*. Prague: Jihočeská Univerzita v Českých Budějovicích.

Rosch, Eleanor. 1978. "Principles of categorization". In Eleanor Rosch and Barbara B Lloyd (eds.), *Cognition and Categorization*. Hillside: Lawrence Erlbaum, 27–48.

Ruiz de Mendoza Ibáñez, Francisco J. 2007. "High-level Cognitive Models". In Krzysztof Kosecki (ed.), *Perspectives on Metonymy*. Frankfurt: Peter Lang, 11–30.

Ruiz de Mendoza Ibáñez, Francisco J. 2010. "Metonymy and cognitive operations". In Réka Benczes, Antonio Barcelona Antonio, and Francisco J. Ruiz de Mendoza Ibáñez (eds.), *What is Metonymy? An Attempt at Building a Consensus View on the Delimitation of the Notion of Metonymy in Cognitive Linguistics*. Amsterdam: John Benjamins, 103–24.

Schlücker, Barbara. 2016. "Adjective-Noun compounding in Parallel Architecture". In Pius ten Hacken Pius (ed.), *The Semantics of Compounding*. Cambridge: Cambridge University Press, 178–91.

van Langendonck, Willy. 2007. *Theory and Typology of Proper Names*. Berlin: De Gruyter.

van Langendonck, Willy and Mark van de Velde. 2016. "Names and grammar". In Carole Hough (ed.), *Oxford Handbook of Names and Naming*. Oxford: Oxford University Press, 17–38.

Warren, Beatrice. 1978. *Semantic Patterns of Noun-Noun Compounds*. Göteborg: Acta Universitatis Gothoburgensis.

Isabel Balteiro

'Fashion'-based (pseudo-)Anglicisms in Spanish Women's Fashion Magazines

1. Introduction

The global prestige and dominance of the English language have facilitated and contributed to the so-called "Anglicization" of European languages (see Görlach 2001, 2002a, 2002b; Fischer & Pulaczewska 2008, De Houwer and Wilton 2011, Furiassi, Pulcini, & Rodríguez González 2012: 3) and other world languages (Anderman & Rogers 2005, Crystal 2012, Price 2014, Ai & You 2015) at different linguistic levels. The lexical component of the language, that which evolves most quickly, is apparently the most commonly affected and probably also where the foreign influences are most evident. That is the case of Spanish in general and in specialized or professional languages. Spanish has largely borrowed English terms with or without a real lexical need, as English loanwords are highly appreciated and associated to prestige, to the point that sometimes anglicisms and false anglicisms either displace or replace native units.

In the language of fashion, anglicisms are most visible, where their adoption is linked to "coolness" but also sometimes to the rapid advances and modernization of fashion and the incapacity of languages to cope with the speed with which extralinguistic realities change. Similarly, false anglicisms (see Furiassi 2010, Rodríguez González 2013, Gottlieb & Furiassi 2015) are also particularly salient in fashion language (see Balteiro & Campos 2012, Balteiro 2014, Balteiro 2018), as we shall explain below. Following our previous research (e.g. Balteiro 2011, Balteiro 2014, Balteiro 2018, Balteiro & Campos 2012, Campos & Balteiro 2020) and our awareness of the predominance of anglicisms and false anglicisms in fashion in Spanish, as well as the comparatively scarce number of studies on either this specialized language in general or the impact of English on it in different world languages, this work explores the adoption and adaptation of the English form *fashion* in Spanish fashion-specialized magazines discourse.

Although fashion is a widely explored area of knowledge (see, amongst others, Barthes 1983; Damhorst, Miller-Spillman & Michelman 1999; Flügel 1930; O'Hara 1986), the language of fashion itself is still under-researched, despite works like Balteiro (2011, 2014, 2018, 2021), Balteiro and Campos (2012), Campos and Balteiro (2020), Díez-Arroyo (2015, 2016a, 2016b), and Lopriore and Furiassi (2015). The study that follows attempts to contribute to the literature on this field by analyzing the use of the term *fashion* in Spanish fashion magazines.

Based on a sample of over four million words from the Spanish edition of the internationally-recognized magazine *Cosmopolitan*, this study explores the uses of *fashion* in Spanish and its competing Spanish form, *moda*. It aims at identifying and describing its nominal functions but also at discovering other pseudo-English uses of the word *fashion* in Spanish. First, we briefly review the Spanish linguistic attitudes towards anglicisms with special attention to the fashion jargon (section 2). Then, the use and importance of false anglicisms in fashion in Spanish is reviewed (section 3). Finally, the empirical study (section 4) focuses on the already mentioned borrowing of *fashion* in specialized women fashion magazines: both the direct incorporation of English genuine uses and also new non-genuine, apparent English uses of the form *fashion* that appear in Spanish, as well as the competing forms *moda*, *de moda*, *a la moda*, etc., in order to determine whether the English unit (*fashion*) has replaced or displaced the native Spanish element (*moda*) in general or in particular cases and combinations.

2. Anglicisms in the Spanish language of fashion

Despite the resistance exerted by the Real Academia Española (RAE, Spanish Royal Academy) and scholars like Lorenzo (1996) or Pratt (1997), who defended linguistic purity and the coinage and use of exclusively native elements, Spanish speakers have always been attracted by English and, hence, eager to accept and integrate English borrowings.

This tendency has been on the increase from the 20th century onwards, due to English globalisation, socio-cultural and educational advances, the mass media and, more recently, social media. However, as Balteiro and Campos (2012: 239–240) note, the adoption of anglicisms is also highly dependent on the users' self-projection and their educational, social and even professional backgrounds.

In the language of fashion in Spanish, for example, English terms and even phrases are expected and conceived of as a positive sign of "coolness" or prestige, which, on the one hand, results in more attention by either the products' potential buyers or magazine readers, and, on the other, their use contributes to an in-group feeling. Sometimes anglicisms fill in actual or perceived lexical gaps in the Spanish language (e.g. 'jeggins', 'clutch', 'vestidos *cupcake*', or 'zapatos *pin-pumps*'), either because the new product or trend is immediately imported without time for a linguistic equivalent or also because, as Phillipson (2003: 72) puts it, "the foreign name is simply a must, as it implies a positive connotation for the special trade". Furthermore, as Balteiro and Campos (2012: 239–240) mention, there are also other motivations for the incorporation of anglicisms in the language of fashion in Spanish, namely, (1) anglicisms may refer to new notions for which Spanish has no equivalent and, consequently, a lexical need actually exists (e.g. *jersey*); (2) anglicisms contribute to lexical convergence and homogenisation among young generations, business people and anyone who may be really keen on fashion (e.g. use of *coolhunter* instead of the "genuinely" Spanish *cazatendencias*); (3) anglicisms also achieve greater precision and economy than Spanish terms or expressions, which tend to be longer (e.g. *jeans* for 'pantalones vaqueros'); (4) the English language itself is a trendsetter; and (5) the use of English "serve[s] to stimulate the reader's feelings and to create a pleasant mood of cosmopolitanism" (Haarmann 1986: 110). Apart from that, we agree with Onysko and Winter-Froemel (2011: 1551–1553) that "even in cases of incontrovertible duplication, the loanword is seen as introducing meaning nuances that eventually differentiate it from the native word", such as accuracy and specificity of meaning (Cabré 1999: 74).

As regards fashion magazine language, the use of anglicisms also obeys to specific and justified reasons. In addition to the cosmopolitan feeling just mentioned, Lopriore and Furiassi (2015: 199) argue that it is "definitely polysemous, connotative, emotional and persuasive, almost like the language of advertising", and as "an integral part of the fashion industry" is characterized by "the plurilingual and multicultural codes of influential stylists and designers" (Lopriore & Furiassi 2015: 199). Furthermore, journalists specializing in fashion write for informative and persuasive purposes for a non-specialist but highly familiarized, fashion conscious and/or "fashion-addicted" readership. These readers, most often women, who tend to have a taste for the different and the cool, are captivated through the use of attractive and catchy language and images, which involves using terms in foreign languages, mainly from English. Sometimes these terms, basically anglicisms but even false anglicisms may even replace or displace native lexical elements (e.g. *blazers* for 'americanas', *oversize* for 'de gran tamaño').

3. False Anglicisms in the Spanish language of fashion

The terminology and/or vocabulary of the fashion jargon in Spanish comprehends not only words created by lexicogenetic processes but also pure (in)direct borrowings (incorporating either words in their original form or adapted to Spanish), or either new forms and senses which "imitate" English forms or meanings, generally known as false anglicisms (e.g. *dermolifting* or 'todas las *it*'). Such false anglicisms, or words with an English appearance that are found in languages other than English, but which either do not exist as such or have different meanings in English, have been studied under a variety of labels. Besides the label "false anglicisms" (Lorenzo 1996, Pratt 1997, Furiassi 2003), these words are also referred to as "pseudoanglicisms" (Alfaro 1970, Carstensen 1980, Gómez Capuz 2001, Görlach 2002a, 2002b, Onysko 2007), and "apparent Anglicisms" (Fanfani 1991, amongst others).

To date, the most detailed classification of false anglicisms is that proposed by Furiassi (2010: 38 ff.), who lists a total of eight types: autonomous compounds (*recordman*), autonomous derivatives (*footing*), compound ellipses (*smoking*), clippings (*relax*), semantic shifts (*mister*), eponyms (*pullman*), toponyms (*sandwich*), and generic trademarks (*rimmel*). However, this taxonomy may be subject to changes depending on the language and data under study. In fact, in our study below new pseudo-English uses identified for the word *fashion* in Spanish do not actually correspond to any of these categories.

Research on false anglicisms is scarce but also problematic, due to (1) the fragmentation of lexicographical research in various languages; (2) the conflicting identification of some anglicisms, especially because particular elements behave differently in different languages and, therefore, may require language-specific analysis, but also because (3) in many cases a European language different from English (in fashion usually French) has acted as the intermediary language and as a vehicle for dissemination of the lexical forms. Thus, in the Spanish language of fashion and beauty, examples of false anglicisms which were coined in French and then were adopted by Spanish users can be found, e.g. *beauty case* (equivalent to English "toilet kit" or "make-up kit"). Some works have already paid attention to these mutual influences between languages (Anderman & Rogers 2005, Fischer & Pułaczewska 2008, Gnutzmann & Intemann 2008, Rosenhouse & Kowner 2008), but still much remains to be researched about the role of intermediary languages and, hence, the actual origin or source language of false anglicisms, which sometimes may also be common to the multiple manifestations of a form in different languages. Therefore, apart from language specific studies like the present one, multilingual analyses are called for. In this chapter, however, we explore and analyse the anglicism *fashion* and also its non-nominal pseudo-English uses in Spanish.

4. The study: The use of *fashion* in Spanish fashion magazines

4.1 Objectives and methodology

On the basis of the hypothesis that the term *fashion* has displaced the native Spanish word *moda* in the language of fashion magazines in Spanish, this study intends to corroborate this idea but also analyse and describe the use, adaptation and integration of the English element in this type of discourse. The analysis is based on the examples manually extracted from a sample of approximately 4,128,000 words obtained by compiling 34 issues, corresponding to years 2015 up to 2021 (both included), of the internationally acknowledged fashion magazine *Cosmopolitan* in its Spanish edition.

4.2 Discussion of results

The analysis of the data obtained has refuted our hypothesis as it revealed that, despite the apparently frequent and marked use of the term *fashion*, this has not displaced or replaced the native Spanish word *moda* in fashion magazines in Spanish. In fact, in our sample, 918 examples of *moda* have been identified compared to 152 uses of the term *fashion*, which means that 85.79 % of the occurrences are examples of the Spanish word while only 14.20 % are occurrences of *fashion*. These results were somehow unexpected as it has often been argued that "the pervasive use of English terms in the field of fashion is more than evident in specialized fashion magazines, probably because they are addressed to a female readership who are ardent fashion and trends followers and for whom Anglicisms exercise attraction and contribute a sense of prestige, modernity and coolness" (Balteiro 2018: 26).

In spite of this relatively low frequency of occurrence of the English unit (especially if compared to the competing Spanish form), the uses and distribution of both elements as well as the forms and uses adopted by the anglicism are worth examining. In general, and also contrary to our expectations, pseudo-English uses of *fashion* (54.6 %), where this anglicism has acquired an attributive or adjectival use, are more frequent than the direct use of unadapted borrowed noun in isolation and within complex loan constructions. Apart from those, very occasionally, *fashion* is also used in our study in adjectival functions modifying Spanish nouns (e.g. "un templo *fashion*"), probably due to analogy with English constructions in which *fashion* continues to be a noun, despite its modifying function. As we shall explain, *fashion* is first directly incorporated into Spanish but later it has undergone different degrees of graphical, morphologic and syntactic adaptation, showing interesting variable forms and contexts (see Table 1).

Anglicism	in whole English constructions	Isolated noun or coordinated with another noun		4		53	69
		Noun phrase or compound	*fashion* as Head noun	5			
			fashion as modifier	42			
		Prepositional or adverbial phrase		2			
	within a Spanish phrase	*fashion*$_N$ as postmodifier in a Spanish noun phrase			16		
False Anglicism	Partially converted adjective, postmodifying Spanish nouns			51			83
	Fully converted adjective	Prefix + *fashion*$_{ADJ}$		7	24	32	
		Adverb + *fashion*$_{ADJ}$		16			
		Adjective + *fashion*$_{ADJ}$		1			
		fashion coordinated with other adjectives		4	8		
		fashion inflected for the plural		1			
		fashion in a comparative construction		1			
		fashion in a Spanish-like adjectival use within an English phrase		2			
TOTAL				152			

Table 1: Summary of *fashion* uses and contexts in Spanish fashion magazines.

4.2.1 *Non-adapted nominal uses of* fashion *in Spanish*

In 69 examples (45.39 %) out of the 152 occurrences of *fashion* in our corpus, this term has been directly borrowed from English and used as such in nominal functions, that is, *fashion* works as either the head noun or as a modifier in a noun phrase. Thus, in 4 non-adapted occurrences

(2.63 % of the total; 5.8 % of the true anglicisms) *fashion* is used as head noun in isolation or coordinated with other nouns such as *shopping* or *beauty¹*, as in:

- FASHION. Para las más atrevidas. [*Cosmopolitan*01/2018:33].
- Fashion & Shopping [*Cosmopolitan*01/2014:9, 34].
- He aquí los cinco imprescindibles *beauty & fashion* de este mes para subir tu *sexy*. [*Cosmopolitan*09/2016:166].

Similarly, *fashion* also appears in 5 examples (3.28 %; 7.24 % of the true anglicisms) as head noun in constructions directly taken from English, namely, in the phrase *fast fashion* (4 examples; 2.63 % or 5.8 % of the true anglicisms), and in the noun phrase "20th-century fashion", as shown below:

- «Les cuesta porque su modelo es el de *fast fashion,* pero, como la sociedad, también se están planteando la necesidad ser más sostenibles». [*Cosmopolitan*01-02/2021:35].

It is worth commenting here that, despite the high level of familiarity of Spanish fashion magazine readers with English anglicisms and, henceforth, with English or English specialized terms, in some cases like the following there is a translation of the English phrase:

- 20TH-CENTURY FASHION (LA MODA DEL SIGLO XX) [*Cosmopolitan*09/2016:163].

Apart from those instances where the anglicism *fashion* acts as head noun, 42 cases (27.63 %; 60.86 % of the true anglicisms) in which it functions as a modifier within a whole English noun phrase have also been identified, as in *fashion blogger, fashion lover, fashion business, fashion victim, fashion trends, fashion system, fashion ilustrators,*

---

1   Only 3 examples are shown here to avoid repetition of identical cases. Nevertheless, where there is some kind of difference (e.g. use of italics vs normal type) similar instances are included to display variety.

fashion book, fashion film, fashion sharing, fashion shows, fashion tips, fashion weeks, fashion news, fashion box, fashion clubbing, etc:

- Yo siempre comento que soy *fashion blogger,* que es como empecé y que es lo que me ha traído hasta aquí. [*Cosmopolitan*11/2019:102].
- ¿Qué le puedo regalar a una 'fashion lover'? [*Cosmopolitan*01/2020:76].
- Pero tengo amigas de verdad en el *fashion business,* . . . [*Cosmopolitan*07/2017:91].
- Las ediciones especiales de 'Good Girl' son el sueño de toda 'fashion victim' [*Cosmopolitan*12/2020:68].
- Respecto a la moda, reconoce que no es una *fashion victim,* aunque le fascina: «Siempre me ha encantado, pero hasta ahora no la había entendido. Estoy cambiando mi forma de vestir, jugando y encontrando mi estilo». [*Cosmopolitan*12/2021:92].
- PARA 'FASHION ADDICTS' [*Cosmopolitan*07/2018:27].
- Fashion Musts [*Cosmopolitan*01/2014:184].

In these examples, *fashion* is modifying a head noun that follows it, but that modification actually occurs in English, and the whole unit, be this a noun phrase or a compound noun, is directly borrowed into Spanish. Note also that, despite the already mentioned high degree of integration of English in Spanish fashion magazines and the familiarity of their readers with the English language, English loans tend to be marked or highlighted in different ways. Accordingly, in the previous examples there is some alternation between the use of italics and quotation marks to highlight the English borrowing. Exceptionally there are some cases, like "Fashion Musts" above, where no italicization or quotation marks are used because the phrase is used as a headline in one of the magazine sections.

Finally, *fashion* is also found as head of a noun phrase within an English prepositional or adverbial phrase. Hence, as above, it is the whole construction that is borrowed and not only the term *fashion* itself. Two examples of this (1.31 %; 2.89 % of the true anglicisms) have been identified in our sample:

- BUSINESS OF FASHION (BOF) Mariana Portocarrero, colaboradora Conocida como la biblia de la moda. ¡Ya está todo dicho! [*Cosmopolitan*04/2019:114].

- 'INSIDE FASHION' Imran Amed, cofundador de *BOF,* la biblia de la moda en versión audio, es el alma de este programa, . . . [*Cosmopolitan*04/2019:115].

4.2.2 *Syntactically adapted use of* fashion *as modifier in a Spanish noun phrase*

The term *fashion* is also found in 16 examples (10.52 %; 23.2 % of the true anglicisms) where it functions as a modifier of a Spanish noun. In such cases the term is syntactically adapted to the Spanish grammar, postmodifying the noun, rather than in a premodifier position as it would be in English. Amongst others ("cine *fashion*", "portal *fashion*", "noticias *fashion*", "una duda *fashion*", "plataformas de suscripción *fashion*", "alerta 'fashion' " or "sarao *fashion*"), the following were identified:

- Convierte tu dormitorio en un templo *fashion,* un espacio privado donde exhibir tu ropa y tu estilo con productos que celebran la individualidad y la creatividad. [*Cosmopolitan*03/2018:29].
- Hoy, el mundo *fashion* sale a la caza y captura de esos rostros que triunfan en la red para convertirlos en embajadores de sus firmas, siguiendo un modus operandi muy diferente al de las campañas tradicionales, pero con el mismo fin: convertir un producto en must have en cuestión de horas. [*Cosmopolitan*04/2016:28].
- Una modelo, dos asesoras y dos diseñadoras analizan cómo ha afectado este fenómeno al universo *fashion.* [*Cosmopolitan*11/2020:34].

These examples, especially in the latter two, show (almost) collocations of *fashion* as modifier of other nouns such as "mundo" or "universo", which may explain the use of only italics to highlight the English word and attract readers' attention. Unlike these, in other less frequent combinations the word *fashion* appears within inverted commas, as in the following four examples:

- **ALERTA 'FASHION'.** SE LLEVAN LOS CALCETINES POR ENCIMA DE LOS 'LEGGINGS' [*Cosmopolitan*03/2021:40].
- Seis consejos para empezar tu proyecto 'fashion' [*Cosmopolitan*04/2021:39].

- ¿Pensando en tu próxima inversión 'fashion'? [*Cosmopolitan*03/2017:126].
- HERENCIA 'FASHION' [*Cosmopolitan*03/2019:26].

While the collocation "mundo *fashion*" appears only once in our data, the corresponding Spanish combination "mundo de la moda" is present in 37 examples, which clearly indicates that the whole purely Spanish construction is not only more frequent but also that the latter is not replaced by the former. Unlike this, "universo *fashion*" is apparently more frequent (4 examples) than the Spanish "universo de la moda" (2 instances), however, this difference is not significant.

4.2.3 *Pseudo-English uses of* fashion

Fashion in English may be an uncountable or a countable noun, indicating either the area of activity that involves styles of clothing and appearance, or a style of clothing or a way of behaving that is popular at a particular time, respectively. Furthermore, this noun may also act as modifier to mean or refer to the latest or most admired style of clothes, accessories, etc. However, *fashion* in English has not yet acquired an adjectival function and, therefore, it is neither used with the meaning of 'cool' or 'fashionable' nor does it replace such words. Spanish, however, has first borrowed and adopted this noun and then it has syntactically and semantically extended its use to adjectival functions, a phenomenon that is often known as conversion, zero-derivation or functional shift (on this see, amongst others, Balteiro 2007). More importantly, as far as our data is concerned, the number and percentages of pseudo-English uses of *fashion* overcome actual English uses, that is, cases where *fashion* functions as a true (non-adapted) anglicism. Apparently, there seems to be a preference for using the Spanish noun *moda* in specific contexts where professional issues are referred to and to limit the use of the anglicism and, particularly, the false anglicism (adjectival uses) to specific contexts such as descriptive ones where the attention of the reader is called for.

Accordingly, there are 83 occurrences of *fashion* acting as an adjective (54.6 % of the instances of this word in the sample), either in predicative or attributive position, modifying nouns, combined with prefixes which provide an intensifying meaning, being modified by adverbs, or coordinated with other adjectives, as explained below.

4.2.3.1 *fashion:* an adjective modifying nouns

The sample contains 51 examples (33.55 %; 61.44 % of the adjectival or pseudo-English uses) of *fashion* functioning as an adjective modifying Spanish nouns related to clothes and accessories, people or other referents such as 'paseos' [walks], 'mundo' [world], 'universo' [universe], 'armada' [navy], or 'romance' [romance], amongst others. No consistent style seems to be observed regarding the use of inverted commas and italics in *fashion*, though the preference is italics. Note that in examples where the Spanish noun appears in the plural, the adjective *fashion* remains, however, invariable (see 'paseos *fashion*' or 'sueños 'fashion'' below). This follows the tendency of actual anglicisms belonging to the adjective word-class, as in 'camisas extra-large' or 'bolsos oversize'.

CLOTHES & ACCESSORIES

- Ahora son un accesorio 'fashion' más. Remata tu 'outfit' con unas vintage como estas [*Cosmopolitan*02/2014:36].
- Puedes combinarlas con faldas de piel sintética y gorros y bufandas *fashion*. [*Cosmopolitan*11/2020:35].

PEOPLE

- SCOOPS. Para chicas *fashion*. [*Cosmopolitan*08/2018:6].

OTHER

- Ideales para paseos *fashion*. [*Cosmopolitan*08/2019:27].
- Encuentra la caja de tus sueños 'fashion'. Las propuestas para estrenar cada mes ropa o accesorios y cambiarlos al siguiente se multiplican. Aquí tienes algunas de las más exitosas. [*Cosmopolitan*01-02/2021:35].
- Seguimos su estela *fashion* durante una jornada [*Cosmopolitan*10/2014:102].
- Las deportivas (AKA sneakers) llegaron para quedarse en el universo *fashion* y ahora se llevan hasta con vestidos de cóctel. Eso sí, que sean blancas y estén relucientes. [*Cosmopolitan*04/2016:50].

- Para encontrar inspiración, nada como dar la vuelta al mundo 'fashion'. En estas vacaciones... ¡síguenos! [*Cosmopolitan*07/2019:42].
- La armada *fashion* más guerrera y puntera es la que se viste de marrón, verdes y cueros. [*Cosmopolitan*09/2016:31].
- Para compensar el frenético ritmo del ADE, lánzate a descubrir los barrios de Ámsterdam: el bohemio De Pijp, el *fashion* Jordaan... sin olvidar el de los museos (piérdete en el Rijksmuseum o en el Stedelijk Museum). [*Cosmopolitan*09-10/2021:135].

4.2.3.2 *fashion:* an adjective modified by intensifying prefixes, adverbs and other adjectives

Thirty-two examples (21.05 % of the total examples of *fashion* in the sample; 38.55 % of the pseudo-English uses) appear in which *fashion* has been fully converted to adjective, functions as an adjective and is modified by other forms, which corroborates its status as an adjective. Thus, apart from 8 cases that will be explained in sections 4.2.3.3 and 4.2.3.4, the following cases were identified in our data: 7 examples of *fashion* adjective with an intensifying (attached or non-attached) prefix (namely, *super-* and *ultra-*), as well as 16 occurrences of *fashion* modified by a Spanish intensifying adverb (e.g. *más*). Like any other adjective, *fashion* may also be modified by another adjective; only one example was present in our data, as shown below.

Prefix + *fashion*$_{ADJ}$

- Hay diseños muy originales y *superfashion* que se adaptan a tu cara, [...]. [*Cosmopolitan*10/2019:35].
- 'ULTRAFASHION' [*Cosmopolitan*12/2020:127].
- una manicura super *fashion* que llene tus uñas de color. [*Cosmopolitan*02/2014:168].

Adverb + *fashion*$_{ADJ}$

- Los trajes de sirena son más *fashion* que nunca [...] [*Cosmopolitan*09/2018:119].
- 52 THE LOOK. Toma nota de lo más *fashion* en complementos. [*Cosmopolitan*10/2018:10].

- La negra queda ideal de día y de noche, combinada con tus looks de fiesta más *fashion* [*Cosmopolitan*09/2020:27].

Adjective + *fashion*$_{ADJ}$

- El color violeta invade el Pantone y todo tipo de prendas y complementos. ¿El top *fashion*? Llevarlo en *total look*. ¿Te atreves? [*Cosmopolitan*12/2016:42].

4.2.3.3 fashion: **an adjective coordinated with Spanish adjectives, modifying Spanish nouns or in comparative constructions**

Within the 32 examples of undoubtful full conversion of *fashion* to adjective and apart from those described in the preceding section, *fashion* is found in coordination with other adjectives such as 'eco' or 'cómoda' (see below), but there are other rare examples which clearly show the conversion, by inflecting for plural like the Spanish noun to which it modifies. This is a remarkable and highly unusual instance not only for its full conversion to adjective but also for its adaptation to Spanish plural inflection, which does neither occur in English, where the adjective category is invariable, nor in non-adapted anglicisms in Spanish.

- Cómoda sí, pero *fashion* también, por favor, ¡que es fin de año! [*Cosmopolitan*11/2020:40].
- Con la nueva temporada anímate a cambiar de filosofía. *Be* eco! Y *fashion* al Besides those, there is another instance which is worth mismo tiempo. [*Cosmopolitan*03/2014:30].
- Captura y guarda tus inspiraciones *fashions* con un clic. Después puedes acceder a ellas on y offline. [*Cosmopolitan*04/2014:34].

Besides those, there is another instance which is worthcommenting on:

- 'Fashion' como 'Cruella'

La villana de Disney, encarnada por Emma Stone, inspira la línea Cruella de Havaianas, con complementos para sentirte tan cool como este personaje.

Clutch 'Cruella'
Havaianas (17,90 €) [*Cosmopolitan*07-08/2021:14].

In this case, *fashion* is an adjective meaning 'cool' that compares or identifies some accessories, in particular, clutches, with/to Cruella who is also 'fashion'.

4.2.3.4 fashion: a Spanish-like adjectival use in English phrases

In addition to the preceding, our sample has revealed the existence of other pseudo-English uses in which *fashion* examples may even be considered as partially converted adjectives, that is, forms which are both syntactically and semantically half-way between noun uses and adjectival ones. Thus, the two cases below, where *fashion* occupies the typical position of a Spanish adjective modifying a noun, though semantically closer to noun reference, have been identified:

- UN DETALLE. Una funda de móvil o un llavero con forma de muñeco colgado del bolso son una manera simple y muy discreta de implementar este hit fashion en tu outfit. [*Cosmopolitan*01/2018:42].
- David Luquin, profesor de Emprendimiento en el ISEM y director de Atelier by ISEM, considera que el modelo de renting fashion puede funcionar muy bien «porque nos empieza a pesar en el armario toda esa ropa que no nos ponemos. [*Cosmopolitan*01-02/2021:34].

5. Conclusions

As argued in other works (see, for example, Balteiro 2018), Anglicisms and pseudo-Anglicisms do not seem to be considered as threats to the purity of the fashion language. However, despite the first impression obtained when having a first look at any fashion magazine in Spanish, the present study has revealed a very different reality. In this case, the anglicism *fashion*, which seems to be ubiquitous in women fashion magazines, is not so frequent. Thus, after analysing the use, frequency and distribution of the Spanish term *moda* and the English equivalent *fashion*, the data in our sample revealed that *fashion* is still far from displacing or replacing *moda*. In fact, there seems to be a tendency to

maintain the most extended, traditional and popular uses of the term
moda in expressions such as "la moda", "las modas", "directora/editora/
diseñadora/. . . de moda", or constructions formed by noun + 'de (la)
moda' (e.g. "consejos de moda", "grito de moda", "marca de moda",
"historia de la moda", "mundo de la moda", "sector de la moda", "sím-
bolo de la moda", . . .) or verb + 'a la moda' (e.g. "estar a la moda",
"dedicarse a la moda", "vinculadas a la moda", "ir a la moda", etc.).
That is, while *moda* is maintained when referring to the fashion profession, industry and/or sector, the anglicism *fashion* is apparently
preferred in whole borrowed English constructions, but mainly in new
innovative adjectival uses to describe products or to refer to something
that is 'cool' or 'fashionable'.

Furthermore, even though there does not seem to be a full and
rigid complementary distribution, it is also quite clear that in nominal uses the term *moda* is preferred, while *fashion* has acquired new
pseudo-English uses in Spanish. Accordingly, *fashion* has been converted into an adjective to describe "fashionable" or "cool" clothes,
accessories, etc., although other partially equivalent forms such as
"puesto de moda", "de moda", etc. also exist in Spanish. Nevertheless,
in this case, the adjectival use of the English form is more frequent. In
general, there seems to be a progressive and increasing incorporation
of the anglicism from the use of the direct unadapted borrowing in isolation or within whole English constructions, where *fashion* functions
as modifier of a noun, to its more frequent adaptation and conversion to
an adjective as in "Cómoda sí, pero *fashion* también, por favor, ¡que es
fin de año!" [*Cosmopolitan*11/2020:40].

Our study has also disclosed that the Spanish fashion language displays a range of possibilities as regards different degrees of morphological and syntactic adaptation, and pseudo-English uses, functions and
forms apparently "imitating" actual English models, as shown in the
preceding sections. Probably to call readers' attention, despite the general high degree of integration and readers' familiarity with the form
fashion in both its adjectival and nominal uses, it most often appears as
a graphically marked term. Italics, inverted commas and even capital-
ization have been displayed in the examples studied, which is not rare
as (graphic) markedness tends to be intrinsic to any borrowed item.

This study does not exhaust the analysis of the term *fashion* in both its nominal and adjectival uses in fashion magazines discourse in Spanish. In fact, it would be interesting to compare and contrast the uses of *moda, fashion, fashionable* and *cool* in a future study in order to determine whether some fixed patterns, some collocations or the existence of some kind of complementary distribution of the terms actually exists.

References

Ai, Hayang and Xiaoye You. 2015. The grammatical features of English in an Internet discussion forum. *World Englishes* 34(2): 211–230.

Alfaro, Ricardo. 1970. *Diccionario de anglicismos*. Madrid: Gredos.

Anderman, Gunilla and Margaret Rogers (Eds.). 2005. *In and Out of English: For Better, For Worse?* Clevedon: Multilingual Matters.

Balteiro, Isabel. 2007. *A Contribution to the Study of Conversion in English*. Münster/New York/München/Berlin: Waxmann Verlag.

Balteiro, Isabel. 2011. "A few notes in the vocabulary of textiles and fashion". In Isabel Balteiro (ed.), *New Approaches to Specialized English Lexicology and Lexicography*. Newcastle: CSP, 83–96

Balteiro, Isabel. 2014. The influence of English on Spanish fashion terminology: -*ing* forms. *ESP Today* 2(2): 156–173.

Balteiro, Isabel. 2018. Non-pronominal uses of it: A case study in women's magazines. *Revista de Lenguas para Fines Específicos* 24(1): 18–46.

Balteiro, Isabel. 2021. Metaphorisation in fashion designers' TED Talks. In Mateo, José and Francisco Yus (eds.), *Metaphor in Economics and Specialised Discourse*. Bern: Peter Lang, 257–282.

Balteiro, Isabel and Miguel A. Campos. 2012. False Anglicisms in the Spanish language of fashion and beauty. *Ibérica* 24: 233–260.

Barthes, Roland. 1983. *The Fashion System*. New York: Hill and Wang.

Cabré, M. Teresa. 1999. *Terminology. Theory, Methods and Applications*. Amsterdam: John Benjamins.

Campos, Miguel A. and Isabel Balteiro. 2020. Power and Norm-Setting in LSP: Power and Norm-Setting in LSP: Anglicisms in the Language of Fashion Influencers, *ILCEA* [online], 40: 1–21.

Carstensen, Broder. 1980. Semantische Scheinentlehnungen des Deutschen aus dem Englischen. In Wolfgang Viereck (ed.), *Studien zum Einfluss der englischen Sprache auf das Deutsche / Studies on the Influence of the English Language on German*. Tübingen: Narr, 77–100.

Crystal, David. 2012. *English as a Global Language*. Cambridge: Cambridge University Press.

Damhorst, Mary Lynn, Kimberly Miller-Spillman, and Susan Michelman. 1999. *The Meanings of Dress*. New York: Fairchild.

De Houwer, Annick and Antje Wilton (Eds.). 2011. *English in Europe Today*. Amsterdam/Philadelphia: John Benjamins.

Díez-Arroyo, Marisa. 2015. From the *atelier* to *e-commerce*: A cognitive approach to neologisms in Spanish fashion. *Terminology* 21(1): 51–75.

Díez-Arroyo, Marisa. 2016a. English words as euphemisms in Spanish Fashion. *English Today* 32(3): 30–39.

Díez-Arroyo, Marisa. 2016b. Vagueness: A Loanword's Good Friend. The Case of 'Print' in Spanish Fashion. *Pragmatics* 26(4): 609–629.

Fanfani, Massimo. 1991. Sugli anglicismi nell'italiano contemporaneo. *Lingua Nostra* 52: 11–24.

Fischer, Roswitha and Hanna Pulaczewska (Eds.). 2008. *Anglicisms in Europe: Linguistic Diversity in a Global Context*. Newcastle-upon-Tyne: Cambridge Scholars Publishing.

Flügel, John Carl. 1930. *The Psychology of Clothes*. London: Hogarth Press.

Furiassi, Cristiano. 2003. False anglicisms in Italian monolingual dictionaries: A case study of some electronic editions. *International Journal of Lexicography* 16: 121–142.

Furiassi, Cristiano. 2010. *False Anglicisms in Italian*. Monza: Polimetrica.

Furiassi, Cristiano, Virginia Pulcini, and Félix Rodríguez González (Eds.). 2012. *The Anglicization of European Lexis*. Amsterdam/Philadelphia: John Benjamins Publishing Company.

Gnutzmann, Claus and Frauke Intemann (Eds.). 2008. *The Globalisation of English and the English Language Classroom.* Tübingen: Gunter Narr Verlag.

Gómez Capuz, Juan. 2001. La interferencia pragmática del inglés sobre el español en doblajes, telecomedias y lenguaje coloquial: una aportación al estudio del cambio lingüístico en curso. *Revista electrónica de estudios filológicos* 2. <https://www.um.es/tonosdigital/znum2/estudios/Doblaje1.htm> [accessed 12 January 2022].

Görlach, Manfred. 2001. *A Dictionary of European Anglicisms.* Oxford: Oxford University Press.

Görlach, Manfred. (Ed.). 2002a. *English in Europe.* Oxford: Oxford University Press.

Görlach, Manfred. (Ed.). 2002b. *An Annotated Bibliography of European Anglicisms.* Oxford: Oxford University Press.

Gottlieb, Henrik and Cristiano Furiassi. 2015. "Getting the grips with false loans and pseudo-Anglicisms". In C. Furiassi and H. Gottlieb. (eds.), *Pseudo-English: Studies on False Anglicisms in Europe.* Boston/Berlin: De Gruyter Mouton, 3–33.

Haarmann, Harald. 1986. Verbal strategies in Japanese fashion magazines —a study in impersonal bilingualism and ethnosymbolism. *International Journal of the Sociology of Language* 58: 107–121.

Lopriore, Lucilla and Cristiano Furiassi. 2015. The influence of English and French on the Italian language of fashion: focus on false Anglicisms and false Gallicisms. In C. Furiassi and H. Gottlieb (eds.), *Pseudo-English. Studies on False Anglicisms in Europe.* Berlin: Walter de Gruyter, 197–226.

Lorenzo, Emilio. 1996. *Anglicismos hispánicos.* Madrid: Gredos.

O'Hara, Georgina. 1986. *The Encyclopedia of Fashion.* London: Thames.

Onysko, Alexander. 2007. *Anglicisms in German: Borrowing, Lexical Productivity, and Written Codeswitching.* Berlin: Walter de Gruyter.

Onysko, Alexander and Esme Winter-Froemel. 2011. Necessary loans – luxury loans? Exploring the pragmatic dimension of borrowing. *Journal of Pragmatics* 43(6): 1550–1567.

Phillipson, Robert. 2003. *English-only Europe? Challenging Language Policy.* London: Routledge.

Pratt, Chris. 1997. Anglicisms in the Academy dictionary: 'No pasarán'. *Estudios Ingleses de la Universidad Complutense* 5: 279–295.

Price, Gareth. 2014. English for all? Neoliberalism, globalization, and language policy in Taiwan. *Language in Society* 43(5): 567–589.

Rodríguez González, Félix. 2013. Pseudoanglicismos en español actual. Revisión crítica y tratamiento lexicográfico. *Revista Española de Lingüística (RSEL)* 43(1): 123–170.

Rosenhouse, Judith and Rotem Kowner (Eds.). 2008. *Globally Speaking. Motives for Adopting English Vocabulary in Other Languages.* Clevedon: Multilingual Matters.

Elisa Mattiello

Underwear as overwear: Spatial Particles in English Fashion Compounds

1. Introduction

This study investigates the use of spatial particles as both first and second elements in compounds, with a focus on fashion language. In their contrastive analysis of English and Italian fashion terms, Biscetti & Baicchi (2019) have shown that English nominal compounds that exhibit a location-located semantic structure are far more frequent in English than in Italian. Productive patterns include not only the noun+ noun (N+N) typical structure (*topcoat*), but also the preposition+noun (P+N) structure (*overshoes*), which is quite frequent in the lexicon of fashion (p. 21). In Biscetti & Baicchi (2019), compounds like *overcoat*, *underskirt*, and *topcoat*, analysed from a cognitive perspective within the Idealised Cognitive Models (Ruiz de Mendoza 2007), belong to the "image schemas" type, as they point to the 'location' of the overall out-fit where they are used (Biscetti & Baicchi 2019: 11):

> Image schemas are cognitive mappings that have a schematic structure and are involved in our understanding of spatial relations such as over-under. (Biscetti & Baicchi 2019: 21)

In the present study, English fashion P+N compounds are analysed from a morphological perspective in order to investigate the role of the prepositions in terms of transparency, compositionality, and headedness of the compounds. Secondly, compounds displaying a preposition as first element are explored in terms of their productivity and analogy in the creation of fashion lexicon terms.

Another type of morphological structure investigated in this study is the V+P one, mostly corresponding to nouns converted from phrasal verb constructions (e.g. *push-up*, *cover-up*), or to analogical formations created on the basis of converted phrasal constructions (e.g. *slipover* coined by analogy with *pullover*) (Mattiello 2017). The latter forms are "syntactically exocentric" (Bauer et al. 2013: 454) and not productive in English.

Data are extracted from two fashion websites, namely *Victoria's Secret*, the largest lingerie and clothing retailer in the United States, and *H&M*, the Swedish multinational clothing-retail company known for its fast-fashion clothing for men, women, teenagers, and children. Victoria's Secret serves customers at nearly 1,400 Lingerie and Beauty stores around the globe and H&M operates in 74 countries with over 5,000 stores under the various company brands. Both retailer companies use their websites to promote and advertise their products, ranging from underwear to overwear. The analysis of fashion terms manually selected from these two respective websites will highlight the relevance of spatial particles to the formation of nominal compounds of the P+N type, and less significantly of the V+P type. A lexicographic investigation of these terms in the *Oxford English Dictionary* (OED 1989–2021) will show their actual recognition and the semantic contribution of each constituent. A corpus-based analysis of spatial particles found in the *Corpus of Contemporary American English* (COCA, Davies 2008) will help verify the predominance of particles related to the vertical axis (*under, over*), which in fashion terminology seem to have become productive compound constituents (Bauer 2001; Mattiello 2017).

The article is organised as follows. Section 2 discusses spatial particles and their classification as either affixes or compound constituents. Section 3 outlines the theoretical aspects involved in the categorisation and morphosyntactic/morphosemantic analysis of nominal compounds exhibiting a spatial particle or preposition. Section 4 analyses the set of fashion prepositional compounds selected, both qualitatively and quantitatively, and Section 5 draws some conclusions on their productivity in terms of frequency, transparency, and profitability.

2. Spatial particles

Spatial particles, also known as "locatives of space" (Bauer et al. 2013: 333), represent a heatedly debated topic in main morphological accounts. Scholars do not agree on their status as either affixes or compound constituents and often treat them separately depending on whether they are native or non-native. Marchand (1969), for instance, treats the morphemes *fore-* and *mid-* as prefixes, because they are no longer free morphemes, but considers *over-* and *under-* as first compound constituents in what he calls "combinations with locative particles as first elements" (p. 108). Both Bauer (1983) and Adams (2001) rather consider non-native elements (e.g. *intra-*, *super-*) as prefixes and native ones (e.g. *out-*, *over-*) as the first elements in compounds. By contrast, Lehrer (1995) and Bauer et al. (2013) claim that both native and non-native elements should be treated as prefixes and not as first elements of compounds on the grounds that they show parallels with affixes, both formally and semantically.

Bauer et al. (2013: 40) justify this claim by putting forward two theoretical arguments. First, in line with them some native elements have effects on the argument structure of verbal bases: e.g., in *over-grow* referring to plants which 'grow so as to obscure', *over-* has a locative rather than quantitative meaning (cf. *overbuy*). Second, they claim that affixes show a coherent semantics that is distinct from their corresponding homophonous free forms (Dalton-Puffer & Plag 2000). For instance, the prefix *over-* is homophonous with the preposition *over* in English, but their meanings are not always perfectly coextensive: e.g., the 'excess' meaning of *over-* is much more prominent in the prefix (e.g. *overweight*) than in the preposition. On the other hand, Bauer et al. (2013: 340) claim that prepositions such as *by* or *after* "often show a wider range of meanings than the prefixes". However, when fashion lexicon is concerned, nominal compounds generally display spatial particles whose meaning is strictly locative, as the particles are used to indicate the position of a garment in relation to other garments (*underskirt*) or human body (*backpack*).

Moreover, Bauer et al. (2013: 442) classify forms with a preposition in first position and a verb or adjective in second position (e.g. *output*, *outgoing*) as "non-canonical compounds", i.e. those that are not formed by productively combining two or more bases, claiming that they differ from "canonical" ones in terms of their properties, such as headedness or internal structure.

Another non-canonical morphological structure where spatial particles occur is that of prepositional compounds, i.e. "forms derived by conversion into nouns from phrasal verbs, accompanied by a stress shift" (Bauer et al. 2013: 442), as in *push úp* vs. *púsh-up* (bra) or *pull óver* vs. *púll-over*. In the latter case, the spatial particle *over* seems to be unrelated to the meaning of the preposition in the phrasal verb (*pull over* '(of a vehicle) to move to the side of the road, esp. in order to come to a stop'), as it refers to the fact that a *pullover* is 'a piece of clothing designed to be pulled on *over* the head, or *over* other garments'.

Hence, in fashion compounds, the suitability of spatial particles is particularly related to their semantic transparency (i.e. how the meaning of a spatial particle as compound constituent is related to the main meaning of the same particle used individually) and to their compositionality (i.e. how the meaning of a spatial particle can contribute to the overall meaning of the compound) (cf. Bourque 2014 for 'semantic transparency' and Mattiello & Dressler 2018 for 'compositionality' in analogical compounds).

In this study, both P+N and V+P structures are called 'prepositional compounds', as in the formations analysed spatial particles display the same purely locative meaning as displayed by their homophonous free morphemes (i.e. prepositions). Hence, patterns such as N+N (*top hat, topcoat, tank top*) or V+N (*cross-body*) are excluded from the analysis of this study, because they do not include prepositions (cf. Biscetti & Baicchi 2019). Adjectival compounds having an Adj+N pattern (*high-waist, high-leg*) or adjectival synthetic compounds such as *under-dressed* or *undersized* are likewise excluded as the focus here is on nominal compounds.

3. Theoretical aspects

For the analysis of prepositional compounds having a nominal function the clarification of a number of theoretical aspects connected with compounds and their interpretation is in order.

Subsection 3.1 deals with semantic transparency, compositionality, and morphological headedness, whereas Subsection 3.2 discusses productivity and analogy.

3.1 Semantic transparency, compositionality, and headedness

In compound words, semantic transparency is a concept that is generally viewed as a matter of constituents' meaning. According to Pollatsek & Hyönä (2005: 262), a compound word is defined as "transparent" when its meaning is consistent with the meanings of the constituents. By contrast, it is defined as semantically "opaque" when its meaning cannot be constructed by combining the meanings of the individual constituents. It ensues from this distinction that semantic transparency is a matter of compositionality, i.e. "the meaning of the whole is a function of its parts" (Bourque 2014: 1).

However, Sandra (1990: 550) mentions a fundamental distinction between transparency and compositionality:

> This might be related to a difference between the notions 'transparency' and 'compositionality'. Whereas the former notion refers to the relationship between compound and constituent meanings, the latter refers to the possibility of determining the whole-word meaning from the constituent meanings. (Sandra 1990: 550)

In other words, a compound is transparent when its meaning is related to its constituents' meaning, whereas a compound's meaning is compositional if it can be determined by combining its constituents' meaning.

In this study, the notion of semantic transparency is applied to constituent morphosemantic transparency and viewed in terms of both "meaning relatedness", i.e. how the meaning of a compound constituent word is related to the main meaning of the same word used individually, and "meaning predictability", i.e. how the meaning of a compound constituent word can contribute to the overall meaning of the compound, that is, to its compositionality (Mattiello & Dressler 2018: 70). Hence, in this study it is claimed that a compound is fully compositional when both constituents are morphosemantically transparent and their relation can be regularly predicted.

The constituents I focus on are spatial particles, which may occupy the left-hand position (*underwear*) or the right-hand position (*pullover*) in fashion compounds. Commonly, in English compounds the right-most position is occupied by the compound head, but this is not the case with compounds converted from phrasal verbs, such as the above-mentioned *pullover*, whose interpretation may be more difficult due to lack of transparency/compositionality, as well as to exocentricity.

As far as headedness is concerned, in psycholinguistic studies (e.g. Libben 1998; Gagné 2009) compound processing has been examined in connection with semantic transparency and morphological headedness. For instance, Libben (1998, 2010) has investigated the role of morpho-logical decomposition in the processing of semantically transparent vs. opaque compounds. Similarly, Jarema et al. (1999: 362) have demon-strated that "the semantic transparency of individual constituents, their position in the string, and morphological headedness interact in the processing of compounds" (see also Gagné & Spalding 2014).

However, as remarked in psycholinguistic studies and recently highlighted by Bourque (2014: 2), the binary opposition between trans-parent and opaque is not sufficient to describe compounds. More pre-cisely, the typology elaborated by Bourque (2014) is based on four basic factors, namely: (1) headedness (endo- vs. exo-centricity), (2) com-positionality (i.e. how individual constituents contribute meaning to the whole), (3) implicit semantic relations within compounds, and (4) semantic homogeneity (i.e. the degree of shared meaning between analogically similar compounds).

In his typology, Bourque (2014: 276–291) has proposed a distinc-tion between fully compositional (i.e. fully transparent), weakly com-positional, partially compositional, and non-compositional (i.e. totally opaque compounds). He defines compositionality as "determined according to individual components' meaning in relation to that of the whole" (Bourque 2014: 258). Thus, in his typology, strongly endo-centric compounds can be fully, weakly or partially compositional, whereas only exocentric compounds can be non-compositional.

In the interpretation of fashion compounds, we envisage that seman-tic transparency and compositionality are essential factors, whereas morphological headedness does not generally contribute to the com-pound interpretation, as most fashion compound terms are exocentric (i.e. the syntactic and semantic head is outside the compound and does not coincide with the right-most element). Indeed, while in the N+N fashion compound *topcoat* the head coincides with the right-hand constituent (i.e. it is a type of 'coat'), in the P+N type (e.g. *overcoat*) or in the V+P type (e.g. *pullover*) the head is usually outside the compound.

3.2 Productivity and analogy

Other two theoretical concepts deserving discussion are productivity and analogy. For productivity Rainer (1987) claims that there are several definitions current in the literature, which describes it in terms of: (a) frequency of the output words; (b) frequency of the input category (i.e. available bases); (c) number of words potentially created by a particular process (cf. Aronoff 1976); (d) possibility of forming new words; (e) probability of new words occurring (cf. Aronoff 1983 for "potential" vs. "actual words"); and (f) number of new forms occurring in a specified period of time.

Bauer (2001: 20) more concisely summarises the above criteria by claiming that the three prerequisites for productivity mentioned in the literature are "frequency, semantic coherence and the ability to make new forms" (cf. Plag 1999). He also argues that the notion of productivity should be considered within the dichotomy of synchrony vs. diachrony. In his view, "a morphological process is productive if it can be used to coin new words" (Bauer 2001: 27). Hence, productivity can be measured in terms of, not the potential, but the actual coining of new words.

Another common dichotomy associated with productivity is the distinction between profitability and availability (cf. "profitable" vs. "available" in Carstairs-McCarthy 1992: 37; "rentable" vs. "disponible" in Corbin 1987: 177). The former (i.e. profitability) refers to the extent to which a morphological process "may be used or has been used to produce large numbers of new words" (Bauer 2001: 49). The latter (i.e. availability) refers to the extent to which a morphological process "can be used in the production of new words" (Bauer 2001: 49). A parallel distinction is drawn by Kastovsky (1986: 586) between "the scope of the rule [availability] and its actual utilization in performance [profitability]". In other words, productivity depends on both the availability of a morphological pattern and its actual use to obtain new words.

Another notion related to word-formation and word-creation is analogy (Anttila 2003). Analogy refers to the creation of words based on the similarity with unique model words (surface analogy) or patterns (analogy via schema) (Mattiello 2017). Thus, for instance, the word *outerwear* 'clothing designed to be worn outside other garments' is probably based on *underwear*, which acts as a single precise model in the analogy. Moreover, *under-* is found in a number of other compound nouns related to fashion lexicon. Hence, its productivity has been interpreted by some scholars as an independent status (prefix) (see § 2), rather than as compound constituent. In the present study, *under-* is considered as a recurrent first element in prepositional compounds.

4. Analysis of spatial particles in fashion compounds

In this section prepositional compounds are analysed from a qualitative viewpoint, for their morphological features, and from a quantitative viewpoint, for their productivity and frequency in COCA. Overall, the analysis is meant to investigate the role of spatial particles in prepositional compounds and their relevance to the formation of fashion terms.

4.1 Qualitative analysis of prepositional compounds

This section discusses prepositional compounds on the basis of the spatial particles that they include, either initially (§§ 4.1.1-4.1.4) or finally (§§ 4.1.5-4.1.7). The prepositions are listed in alphabetical order.

4.1.1 Back-

In the OED *back-* is considered a "combining form" (Warren 1990) converted from either the noun *back* or the corresponding adverb/ adjective. In combinations, it indicates 'something of or pertaining to the back, used for or carried on the back', as in *backpack*, which is used in fashion lexicon to refer to a sort of 'small rucksack or musette bag'. The spatial particle *back-*, therefore, is used to form a transparent endocentric compound which refers to a sort of 'pack' (a fashionable bag) to be carried on the 'back'. As a compound constituent, it locates the accessory where it should be worn in relation to the owner's body (see also the noun *back* referring to the body part). By contrast, *back* in *backless* is a nominal base suffixed with *-less* to obtain an adjective, as in the phrase *backless bra* used in fashion language.

4.1.2 Out-

The spatial particle *out-* is used in fashion to form compound nouns with the sense 'exterior, external'. Its use as compound constituent is much rarer than the use of *over-* or *under-* (§§ 4.1.3-4.1.4), as shown by the obsolete nouns † *out-clothing* [1496] and † *out-garment* [1634].[1] In fashion websites it occurs in *outfit*, referring to 'a set of clothes (often including accessories) selected or designed to be worn together'. Since *fit* is also used as a noun for 'a garment that fits' and *out-* refers to 'external' garments, the compound *outfit* can be regarded as transparent and compositional, even if the meaning of the compound is more specific than the meaning contributed by the two constituents.

4.1.3 Over-

The spatial particle *over-* is used in fashion to form compounds with concrete nouns denoting the covering object, medium, etc. as second constituent: e.g., *overcloth* 'an outer garment (obsolete); a cloth placed over or upon something', *overcoat* 'a long, usually warm coat, esp. as worn by a man', *overgarment* 'an outer garment', *overshirt* 'a shirt worn over other garments', and *overshoe* 'a shoe worn over an ordinary shoe, either to provide protection from wet, dirt, cold, etc., or to prevent damage to or soiling of the floor'. Other compounds recorded in the OED include: *over-boot* [1841], *over-sock* [1841], and *over-gaiter* [1860] (all generally in the plural); *over-jacket* [1830], *over-cape* [1894],

---

1   The dates reported in square brackets refer to the first attestation of the nouns in the OED. Definitions are all taken from the OED (1989–2021), online edition, last accessed June 2021.

over-collar [1894], and more recent *over-mitt* [1971] and *over-jumper* [1975].

The spatial particle *over-* generally refers to layers of clothing, and is used in the sense 'worn over or above', 'upper or outer'. In this sense, we find it in *overclothes* or *overclothing*, *overgarment*, *overdress* 'outer clothing; a dress or similar garment designed to be worn over other clothes',[2] *oversleeve* 'an outer sleeve covering the ordinary sleeve of a garment', *overskirt* 'an outer skirt, usually worn over the skirt of a dress', *overshirt*, *overshoe*, *overall* 'a protective outer garment; (now esp.) a loose coat or smock worn to keep the clothes beneath clean',[3] and *overbag* (the latter is not recorded in the OED). The additional semantic features conveyed by *over-* are 'providing warmth' (e.g., in *overcoat*, *over-jacket*) or 'protective' (e.g., in *overshoe*, *over-boot*, *overall*, *overbag*). In the latter case, *overall* and *overbag* protect the clothes or accessories which are beneath, whereas *overshoe* and *over-boot* can protect either what is beneath (shoe or boot) or the soil or floor stepped on by the shoe/boot.

From the morphological viewpoint, it is noteworthy that some of these compounds are endocentric: e.g., in *overshirt* 'a shirt worn over other garments', the second constituent is the compound head, while in *overskirt* 'a skirt worn over the skirt of a dress' it is doubtful whether the second constituent stands for the compound head or not. Others, by contrast, are less transparent, headless, and therefore only partially compositional: e.g., an *overshoe* is not 'a type of shoe', but 'a covering for shoes that is generally hard-wearing and impermeable to moisture'. In *overall*, transparency is even decreased by the ambiguity and generality of the pronoun *all*.

4.1.4 Under-

The opposite spatial particle – i.e. *under-* – is often used in compound names of garments worn under other articles of clothing. The first attestation of such compounds is found in Old English *underhwitel*

---

2   Cf. *overdress* as 'excessively ostentatious dress', where *over-* refers to 'excessive showiness'.
3   Cf. *surtout* 'a man's greatcoat or overcoat', from French.

'undergarment', but *under-* mainly became a common compound constituent in the 16th century, when *undercap, -forebody, -frock, -garment, -girdle*, and *-sleeve* occurred. In these compounds, the spatial particle expresses position with reference to that which is above. The OED also records examples of dated as well as more recent compounds: e.g., † *undercloak* [1611] (obsolete), *underwaist* [1857], *underflannel* [1859], *underbodice* [1873], *underdrawers* [1894], *underslip* [1922], and *undershorts* [1960]. Rarely, this native spatial particle competes with non-native *sub-*, similarly used to form nouns denoting an item of underclothing (e.g. † *subvestment* [1802], *sub-armour* [1858], *subtrousers* [1890]). However, the predominance of *under-* over *sub-* as the first element of compounds is evident in current fashion terms, such as general *underwear* 'underclothing', *underclothes* (the verb *to undercloth* also exists, back-derived from *underclothing*), and *undergarment*, or more specific *underskirt* 'a skirt worn under another, a petticoat', *undervest, undershorts*, and *undershirt*.

All the above-mentioned P+N compounds are exocentric, in that the head of the compound is not included in their constituents. However, they are partially transparent, in that they all refer to 'garments worn under X', where X stands for clothes or articles of clothing, such as shirt, skirt, vest, etc., which are expressed by the second constituent. Therefore, they are also partially compositional, in that the meaning contributed by each compound constituent is essential to the meaning of the whole compound and helps locate the garment where it is exactly worn. The meaning contributed by the preposition *under-* is particularly relevant to the understanding of the type of clothing, which transparently refers to 'underwear'. The importance of the spatial particle is confirmed by the existence of the fashion term *undies* [1906], a diminutive euphemistic abbreviation recorded by the *Online Etymology Dictionary* (2021) for 'women's underwear (or undergarments)'.

A modern compound noun belonging to fashion terminology is *underwire*, which is used to refer to both 'a wire or strap stitched into the underside of each cup of a brassière, to support or shape the breast' (as in *underwire bra*) and 'a brassière with such support'. In the first case, *under-* indicates the position of the 'wire' in relation to the 'brassière', while in the second case, the meaning of the compound is clearly metonymic, i.e. *underwire* refers to the whole brassière.

4.1.5 -On

The spatial particle *-on* is only found in *pull-on* 'a hat or garment that may be pulled on without requiring fastening', converted from the phrasal verb *to pull on* 'to put on, don (a garment, etc.), esp. hurriedly'. The preposition here indicates the position of the hat or garment, i.e. on the wearer's body. Yet, the compound is exocentric and its compositionality is weak, with partial transparency focused on the action ('*pull* the garment *on*') rather than on the referent. The meaning component related to hurry or easiness when putting the garment on is completely opaque and absent from the compound constituents' meaning.

4.1.6 -Over

The spatial particle *-over* is used in a fashion compound obtained from a phrasal verb, i.e. *pullover*. Synonymous with jumper or sweater, *pullover* was originally used in the sense 'a piece of clothing designed to be pulled on over the head', but now it especially refers to 'a knitted garment put on over the head and covering the top half of the body'. Hence, the function of the particle *-over* is to locate the garment in relation to the wearer's body, namely 'over one's head'. The same function is in the synonymous compound *slipover*, obtained from the phrasal verb *to slip over*, by analogy with *pullover*. Actually, the OED describes its origin as a conversion from the adjective *slip-over* 'of a garment: made without an opening at the front, and to be slipped on over the head'. As a noun, it is usually spelt as a solid (not hyphenated) compound used to describe 'a sweater or pullover, usually with a V-neck and no sleeves'. The function of the spatial particle *-over* is again locative, as it refers to the way the garment is worn, i.e. by pulling it over one's head.

Nominal compounds converted from phrasal verbs, such as *pullover* or *slipover*, are headless or exocentric. Thus, their transparency is low, as the components refer to the action performed by the person wearing the garment, but the semantic head 'sweater' or 'jumper' is outside the compound itself. As a result, these compounds are only weakly compositional.

4.1.7 -Up

A deverbal nominal compound containing *-up* is *push-up* 'a bra or similar garment which is padded or underwired to give uplift to the breasts', or 'an accessory inserted into a bra or similar garment to provide such uplift'. In this case, the preposition *-up* found in the converted noun refers to the movement (uplifting) that the type of garment causes to women's breasts when wearing it. A different function is performed by *-up* in *cover-up* 'a high-necked garment, a cover-all', where the compound noun owes its origin to the phrasal verb *to cover up* 'to wrap up so as to conceal'. In this case the particle *-up* describes the position of the garment with respect to all the other garments worn. In both compound nouns, the head is outside. Hence, they are partially opaque and only weakly compositional. The semantic contribution of the particle *-up* is different, but equally significant: i.e., 'a bra which *pushes* or lifts the breasts *up*' and 'a garment which is put *up* and *covers* other garments'.

4.2 Quantitative analysis in my dataset and in COCA

The data collected for the qualitative analysis will be now investigated from the quantitative viewpoint, by considering the number of types that each first or second compound component originates in line with the OED and the websites chosen, and their type/token frequency in COCA. This investigation aims at finding the productivity and analogical nature of spatial particles in the formation of fashion compounds. For the corpus investigation, each of the above particles (see § 4.1) was first searched automatically in COCA (e.g. *back**, **on*), and then relevant lemmas pertaining to fashion lexicon were manually selected for the count of types and tokens.

Table 1 shows the results of my quantitative analysis. Frequency of tokens – raw and normalised (per million words = pmw) in COCA – is provided in the last column of Table 1, in decreasing order. Different spellings (solid or hyphenated) are also reported in the table, the most common first.

Particle	Position	Types in the OED / Fashion websites	Types in COCA	Tokens in COCA
back-	first	1	1	backpack (6,324/6.37)
-on	second	1	1	pull-on (14/0.01)
out-	first	3	1	outfit (10,913/10.99)
over-	first	20	9	overall/over-all (71,452/71.95), overcoat (1,618/1.63), overshoe (49/0.05), overdress (25/0.03), overskirt (16/0.02), overbag (13/0.01), overshirt (13/0.01), overdressing (12/0.01), oversock (12/0.01)
-over	second	2	1	pullover (375/0.38)
under-	first	19	14	underwear/under-wear (8,661/8.77), underpants (1,261/1.27), undershirt (714/0.72), undergarment/under-garments (570/0.57), underclothes (111/0.11), undershorts (91/0.09), undercoat (5/0.05), underskirt (41/0.04), underclothing (35/0.04), underdrawers (21/0.02), undersuit (19/0.02), underdress (13/0.01), underslip (6/0.01), under-boot (5/0.01)
-up	second	2	2	push-up/pushup (830/0.83), suit-up (13/0.01)

Table 1: Frequency of spatial particles in fashion compounds.

Corpus investigation confirms the productivity of spatial particles as initial compound constituents, not only in terms of token frequency (i.e. total number of complex words which exhibit them in COCA), but also in terms of type frequency, and hence of profitability in the creation of different and novel fashion compounds. The figures especially demonstrate the relevance of *over-* (20/9 types) and *under-* (19/14 types) as first compound constituents in fashion lexicon. Even though these compounds are headless, their compositionality and partial transparency help disambiguation. The analogical nature of some of such formations is confirmed by the semantic contribution that spatial particles give: *over-* and *under-* specify the position of a garment, cloth or accessory in relation to other garments, which may be indicative of its usefulness to provide warmth or to protect (*overcoat, overshoe*), or to be worn under other clothes for hiding the body or some body parts (*undershirt, underskirt*).

Table 1 also confirms that the productivity of such particles as second components in compound nouns converted from phrasal verbs is lower, as they are generally confined to one instance (*pull-on*), or analogical creations coined after model words (*slipover* after *pullover*).

5. Conclusions

This study has investigated the role of spatial particles in the formation of fashion nominal compounds. It has selected relevant data from two fashion websites, namely *Victoria's Secret* and *H&M*, which specialise in under- and over-wear.

The two types of compound pattern identified (i.e., P+N and V+P) contain spatial particles either initially or finally. The prepositions used include initial *back-* (e.g. *backpack*), *out-* (e.g. *outfit*), *over-* (e.g. *overcoat*), and *under-* (e.g. *underskirt*), as well as final *-on* (e.g. *pull-on*), *-over* (*pullover*), and *-up* (e.g. *push-up*). The former group generally uses the particle to relate the garment's position to that of other garments, whereas the latter group either uses the preposition to indicate where the garment is worn or to explain its relation with the wearer's body. A morphosemantic investigation has shown that, although most of these compounds are headless and their transparency and compositionality are only partial or weak, their analogical nature and similarity with other compounds in fashion lexicon help meaning disambiguation.

In fashion compounds, endocentricity and full compositionality have proved to be nearly absent, with very few exceptions (e.g. *outfit*). However, the data analysed in this study have shown the importance of two other factors contributing to the compounds' transparency, namely, implicit semantic relations within compounds and semantic homogeneity or the degree of shared meaning between analogically similar compounds (Bourque 2014). These two factors help increase the transparency of fashion compounds, whose semantic relations are often determined by the prepositions having a locative function (e.g. *underskirt* 'a garment which is worn *under* a skirt') and whose similarity with other names for garments or accessories facilitates the association with the model words (e.g. *overbag* based on *overshoe* or *overboot*).

Quantitative results obtained from corpus investigation confirm the frequency of spatial particles as (especially initial) compound constituents and their profitability in fashion terminology, especially in the formation of complex words related to the vertical axis (*underslip*, *oversocks*).

References

Adams, Valerie. 2001. *Complex Words in English*. Harlow: Pearson Education/Longman.

Anttila, Raimo. 2003. Analogy: The warp and woof of cognition. In Brian D. Joseph and Richard D. Janda (eds.), *The Handbook of Historical Linguistics*, 425–440. Oxford: Blackwell.

Aronoff, Mark. 1976. *Word Formation in Generative Grammar*. Cambridge, Mass.: MIT Press.

Aronoff, Mark. 1983. Actual words, potential words, productivity and frequency. *Proceedings of the Thirteenth International Congress of Linguist*, Tokyo, 163–171.

Bauer, Laurie. 1983. *English Word-formation*. Cambridge: Cambridge University Press.

Bauer, Laurie. 2001. *Morphological Productivity*. Cambridge: Cambridge University Press.

Bauer, Laurie, Rochelle Lieber, and Ingo Plag. 2013. *The Oxford Reference Guide to English Morphology*. Oxford: Oxford University Press.

Biscetti, Stefania and Annalisa Baicchi. 2019. Space oddity: What fashion terms can reveal about English and Italian cognitive systems.

In Simona Segre Reinach (ed.), *The Culture, Fashion, and Society Notebook*. Milano/Torino: Pearson-Mondadori, 29–43.

Bourque, Stephen Yves. 2014. "Toward a typology of semantic transparency: The case of French compounds". Unpublished Ph.D. Thesis. Department of French Studies, University of Toronto.

Carstairs-McCarthy, Andrew. 1992. *Current Morphology*. London/ New York: Routledge.

Corbin, Danielle. 1987. *Morphologie dérivationnelle et structuration du lexique*, 2 vols. Tübingen: Max Niemeyer Verlag.

Dalton-Puffer, Christiane and Ingo Plag. 2000. Categorywise, some compound-type morphemes seem to be rather suffix-like: On the status of *-ful, -type,* and *-wise* in Present Day English. *Folia Linguistica* 34(3–4): 225–244.

Davies, Mark. 2008. *Corpus of Contemporary American English* (COCA). Available at https://corpus.byu.edu/coca/ (last accessed 18/06/2021).

Gagné, Christina L. 2009. Psycholinguistic perspectives. In Rochelle Lieber and Pavol Štekauer (eds.), *The Oxford Handbook of Compounding*. Oxford: Oxford University Press, 255–271.

Gagné, Christina L. and Thomas L. Spalding. 2014. Typing time as an index of morphological and semantic effects during English compound processing. *Lingue e Linguaggio* 13(2): 241–262.

H&M, retrievable from https://www.hm.com/ (last accessed 07/05/ 2021).

Jarema, Gonia, Céline Busson, Rossitza Nikolova, Kyrana Tsapkini, and Gary Libben. 1999. Processing compounds: A cross-linguistic study. *Brain and Language* 68: 362–369.

Kastovsky, Dieter. 1986. The problem of productivity in word formation. *Linguistics* 24: 585–600.

Lehrer, Adrienne. 1995. Prefixes in English word-formation. *Folia Linguistica* 29(1–2): 133–148.

Libben, Gary. 1998. Semantic transparency in the processing of compounds: Consequences for representation, processing, and impairment. *Brain and Language* 61: 30–44.

Libben, Gary. 2010. Compound words, semantic transparency, and morphological transcendence. In Susan Olsen (ed.), *New impulses in word-formation*. Hamburg: Buske, 317–330.

Marchand, Hans. 1969. *The Categories and Types of Present-day English Word-formation: A Synchronic-Diachronic Approach.* 2nd edn. München: Beck.

Mattiello, Elisa. 2017. *Analogy in Word-formation: A Study of English Neologisms and Occasionalisms.* Berlin & Boston, MA: De Gruyter Mouton.

Mattiello, Elisa and Wolfgang U. Dressler. 2018. The morphosemantic transparency/opacity of novel English analogical compounds and compound families. *Studia Anglica Posnaniensia* 53: 67–114. DOI: 10.2478/stap-2018-0004.

Online Etymology Dictionary. 2021. https://www.etymonline.com/ (last accessed 02/06/2021).

Oxford English Dictionary Online, 2nd edn./3rd edn. (1989–2021). Oxford: Oxford University Press, http://www.oed.com/ (last accessed 02/06/2021).

Plag, Ingo. 1999. *Morphological Productivity. Structural Constraints in English Derivation.* Berlin/New York: Mouton de Gruyter.

Pollatsek, Alexander and Jukka Hyönä. 2005. The role of semantic transparency in the processing of Finnish compound words. *Language and Cognitive Processes* 20(1/2): 261–290.

Rainer, Franz. 1987. Produktivitätsbegriffe in der Wortbildungslehre. In Wolf Dietrich, Hans-Martin Gauger and Horst Geckeler (eds.), Grammatik und Wortbildung romanischer Sprachen. Tübingen, Gunter Narr, 187–202.

Ruiz de Mendoza, Francisco J. 2007. High-level cognitive models. In Krzysztof Kosecki (ed.), *Perspectives on Metonymy.* Frankfurt: Peter Lang, 11–30.

Sandra, D. 1990. On the representation and processing of compound words: Automatic access to constituent morphemes does not occur. *The Quarterly Journal of Experimental Psychology Section A*, 42: 529–567.

Victoria's Secret, retrievable from https://www.victoriassecret.com/ (accessed 07/05/2021).

Warren, Beatrice. 1990. "The importance of combining forms". In Wolfgang U. Dressler, Hans C. Luschützky, Oskar E. Pfeiffer and John R. Rennison (eds.), *Contemporary Morphology.* Belin/ New York: Mouton de Gruyter, 111–132.

Anna Romagnuolo

The Political Language of Fashion

"as the face is the mirror of the soul, so dress is the index of the mind"
Poor Richard[1]

"Decorating, covering, uncovering or otherwise altering the human form in accordance with social notions" of propriety, beauty, religious or civil solemnity, and challenges to these notions to signal changes in status, have always been a preoccupation of human societies, as observed by Terence Turner (2012: 486), who defines clothing as "the social skin", pinpointing how self-fashioning reveals collective in addition to individual inclinations. The economies of clothing, with its supply chains and selection modalities, display the material, institutional and political culture as well as the psychology of historical populations. Dominant ideologies and forms of resistance and/or of cultural (ri) appropriation have been displayed through dress codes across the globe in every period. History provides many eloquent examples: sanctuary laws limiting social climbing and falling, showing similar features in as distant geographical regions as early modern Europe, the Ottoman empire, Latin America, Ming China and Edo Japan;[2] medieval regulations restricting the movements of lepers and victims of skin diseases,[3] control mechanisms relying on (un)dressing insane paupers in 18th and

---

1   Richard Saunders (1782). "On Dress", *Poor Richard Improved,* (qtd. in Haulman 185).
2   Already existing in ancient Rome, the laws enforced dress codes with the official aim of limiting excess of apparel and the less official purpose of distinguishing social classes maintaining a clear delineation of rank. See on this, Giorgio Riello (2020) and Rebecca Earle (2019).
3   Lepers were compelled to wear a mantle and a beaver-skin hat, or a green gown, or a heart symbol on their clothes, and walk with noisemakers such as a bell or a clapper to be identified and kept at a distance. On this and a wider discussion of medieval dressing, among the many books, the series edited between 2005

19th century lunatic asylums,[4] imperial regimes regulating plantation and slave attire,[5] anti-cross-dressing laws criminalizing non-normative gender expression,[6] Nazis concentration camp prisoners' identity-stripping uniforms and hair shaving,[7] colonial and post-colonial European-style Asian and African dresses aimed at integration and Western derision of cultural appropriation and emulation of European demeanors,[8] and import duties discouraging foreign "superfluities" and

and 2020 by Monica L. Wright, Robin Netherton and Gale R. Owen-Crocker, *Medieval Clothing and Textiles*, published by Boydell & Brewder, and Herbert Norris (1998) and Francoise Piponnier & Perrine Mane (1997).

4   There is plenty of literature on the topic. See John Conoly (1846) on the recommended dresses for patients in lunatic asylums in Britain in the 19th century, where the author admits that "dressing in unbecoming clothing" is "only gratifying to those who impose it", but remarks: "Uniformity of dress is chiefly desirable as a check on escapes" (p. 94). Also useful: Jonathan Andrews (2007a and 2007b), Jane Hamlett & Lesley Hoskins (2013), Vivienne Richmond (2013), and Louise Hide (2014).

5   On Roman slaves' clothing habits see, among many, Richard P. Saller (1998); on colonial slave attire, Robert S. DuPlessis (2012) and the interesting essays by Beverly Lemire (2020), Sophie White (2020) and Miki Sugiura (2020) on slave clothing in North America and South African colonies, in B. Lemire and G, Riello (Eds.) (2020); on fabric trade and colonists' spiritual tension between choosing fashionable items making a sartorial statement and wearing plain dresses to respect Christian modesty, see Kate Haulman (2011).

6   The laws were more frequent in growing frontier towns seeking to attract middle-class families with an image of respectability and, therefore, aimed at discouraging prostitution and homosexuality. See on this, Clare Sears (2015). A comprehensive summary of state rules relating to gender and sexual nonconformity and a focus on the new "purity movement", which arose in America against prostitution and "gender inversion" in the late nineteenth century, is contained in William N. Eskridge (1999).

7   On the effacement of an individual's identify through the forceful removal of personal belongings and clothes, whose replacement was aimed at erasing personality traits and marks of social stratification, Maya Suderland (2013). Equally useful, Tadeuz Iwaszko (2000). On the importance of clothing and prisoners' strategies of survival, also consisting in changes and alterations to the blue-and-white-striped dehumanizing prison uniform, see also Claudia Theune (2018).

8   British reactions to "cultural cross-dressing" and "sartorial tensions" in colonial India are well described in Tara Mayer (2020). On the African appropriation of Western-styled garments after exposure to missions, domestic service in white European households and trade cloth, Karen Tranberg Hansen (2010).

encouraging local fabric manufacture (Haulman 2011). All of these demonstrate the interplay of fashion and politics.

When states' enforced norms proved ineffective or inapplicable, social disapproval set the standard. Mockery of attire, allusions to confused sexual orientation associated with inappropriate outfits, and accusations of chasing the latest fad, levelled especially against women and effeminate men, have been valid means of regulating gender appearance and status politics while disciplining and correcting unconventional self-fashioning and chastising unbecoming, promiscuous behavior.

Fashion has always spoken the dual language of (non)conformity to sartorial traditions and inspired dualism both in terms of production and consumption habits and individual and collective behavior, as proved by the opposite concepts: fast fashion versus slow fashion, fashion-lovers versus alt- and anti-fashion brigades, enfashioning and self-fashioning versus naturism and nudism. Just as in imperial Rome changes in status were displayed through changes in clothes and Roman emperors had to dress in ways that could mediate between conformity to the frugality of their ancestors and the indication of their superior political position, in revolutionary America public attire was also the result of the difficult choice between cultivating conventional eighteenth-century gentility and pursuing a more appropriate republican understatement, which was also encouraged by the difficulty of keeping pace with changes in fashion produced at a physical and metaphorical distance. Hence, during the War of Independence and even more so in the early republican years, public attitude towards fashion revealed two modes of thought: if they aped the European style, women could appear too casual or too "gay" and "tawdry" while men could be considered either flops or victims of frivolous and spendthrift wives; both were frequently accused in local magazines and newspapers with political affiliation of jeopardizing domestic manufacture and trade by preferring foreign fashion items (Haulman 2011: 181–227). However, if they dressed too plainly, especially if political leaders or members of local elites, they were judged inadequate to represent the country. A truly "republican" style signaling political and cultural independence from the old world required sobriety but care,[9] practicality but

---

9   *The Poor Richard Almanac* defined lack of care as "indolent negligence" and
     recommended "neither court nor despise the fashions, but always keep the

elegance, and simplicity but taste to compete with the former mother country and with France, a new ally but old master of "à la mode".[10] And, above all, it required local manufacture displaying fashionability and the capacity to befit the wearer's social status. The double standard particularly affected women, often used as a scapegoat for the problems of the young nation (so that a marriageable girl had to be fashionable enough for good society but modest enough not to scare potential suitors fearing the financial burden of an expensive wife) but did not spare presidential candidates and incumbents, urged to resort to national dressmakers.[11] It reflected a necessity to use clothing as an emblem of people's self-determination, typical of countries reclaiming their national identity and cultural modernization at the end of Colonialism, which has contributed to making fashion complicit with commodity culture and political marketing.

In the 1960s, wearing long hair, beards, blue jeans and colorful, unisex dresses became a symbol of political engagement displayed by numerous social movements fighting racism, sexism, consumerism and militarism, such as hippies and black power, women and gay liberation activists; however, it was also what challenged conformism to gender, race, and class definitions according to the mainstream, traditional Euro-American middle-class standards of respectability.[12] Thus, hair

---

    medium and avoid the extreme". (qtd. in Haulman 185).

10   Rallying cries against spending on foreign imports of fabric, buttons and clothing accessories were frequent in the *Pennsylvania Gazette*, especially in the "Essay on the Means of Promoting Federal Sentiment in the United States, by a Foreign Spectator", which appeared weekly in the newspaper between August and September 1787.

11   George Washington was accused of disregarding the welfare of the country, whose cause of freedom he had fought for, and of hypocrisy for wearing foreign manufactured clothes so that the first president had to wear a suit made of domestic cloth at his inauguration, which was lauded in newspapers as being "so handsomely finished that it was universally mistaken for foreign manufactured superfine cloth", proving, quite ironically, that foreign fashion was still the touchstone. (Cfr. Haulman: 213–214). His choice not only validated national manufacture making a sartorial statement of republican virtue but also provided a model for future presidents.

12   See on this Betty L. Hillman (2015) and Ekle Gaugele and Monica Titton (Eds.) (2019).

and dress styles were again the evidence of the cultural divide in America and elsewhere, being at the same time the symbol of a fight for racial equality, female emancipation and freedom of expression invoked by youth tribes,[13] and of rebellion, gender and class role confusion and sexual promiscuity, which fueled conservatives' political anxieties and working class counterprotests.[14]

In later and recent times, compliance with the mainstream politics and subversion or contestation have continued to be expressed through clothes, accessories and hairstyles: wearing a *qipao* in interwar China was a nationalist sartorial statement just as a Mao suit was a symbol of proletarian unity after the Communist victory in the Chinese civil war; wearing RAR[15] badges meant participating in the anti-racism

---

13   Of course, the '60s subcultures were inspired by earlier movements, linked to the beat writers, the birth of jazz and hip pop, and working-class unrest, which originated fashion expressions such as *Zooties, Hipsters, Bikers, Teddy Boys, Rockers*, the younger siblings of *Ton Up Boys*, and their metaphorical or real but much press-hyped riots with *Mods*. For an overview, Maria C. Marchetti (2020); for more detailed accounts, Dick Hebdige (1979), the first book with a focus on punk and raggae styles, besides hipsters and teddy boys, and Ted Polhemus (1994) on the replacement of high culture by popular culture, validated by street credibility, gained by dressing down or dressing up.

14   As in the so called "hard hat riots", when around four hundred construction workers and nearly eight hundred office workers attacked students protesting against the Vietnam War in New York on May 8, 1970. These counterprotests were generated not only by anti-war activism (as working-class Americans, whose sons were fighting in the war, were angry at privileged college students supporting Vietnamese communists) but also by the gender-ambiguous and sexualized styles of student protestors, menacing their traditional masculine breadwinner look. (Cfr. Hillman 2015). It is worth noting that since then the expression indicating literally the protective hat usually worn by the workers has been used to indicate a person who would cling to his/her nationalistic political ideas, and as a synonymous with white working-class conservative. (Barret 2006: 128).

15   The British Rock Against Racism Movement (RAR) was conceived by its founder, photographer Red Saunders, as a one-off concert against a racist remark (on England becoming a black colony) made by Eric Clapton during his concert in Birmingham in August 1976, but it rapidly became a movement involving black and white designers, writers, actors, musicians and performers committed to creatively fight the rise in populist and explicit racist anti-immigration groups. For nearly ten years, it organized antic-racism activities, mainly gigs, carnivals,

demonstrations of the '70s,[16] while black leather jacket, black shirts and Afro hairstyles were synonymous with the Black Panther uniform. Be it truthful or misleading, the choice of fashion items communicates more than a message of individual taste. It reflects social hierarchies of value, displays individual and collective preferences, reveals conscious or unconscious beliefs about identities, and conveys religious norms, social status, and personal experiences. Hence, a hijab is associated with fundamentalism, a keffiyeh is considered a symbol of Palestinian self-determination and a cross-style swastika an indication of neo-Nazism affiliation. The communicative potential of an item is not only associated with its symbolic selection, but also with its manufacture, shape and label, which can display, hide, or betray quality, (legal, illegal, conventional, innovative, sustainable) production processes, market segment, and related political decisions. Moreover, it speaks through fashion photography, with its potential for mass reproduction and dissemination, illustrating patterns of consumption, culturally determined and space/time-dependent customer attractiveness (which allows a further distinction of folk or regional costume from transnational and cross-fertilized dresses, and of seasonal from evergreen apparel).[17] Finally, it speaks through its lexicon, not only with the quantity of words supplied to everyday and specialized language - from the oldest (5,500-year-old) moccasin made of cowhide found in

---

live tours, released music and published a funzine entitled *Temporary Hoardings*.

16   On the role of fashion in political militancy, see Djurja Bartlett (Ed.) 2019, with an interesting chapter on dress and nation states and a detailed account of the Black Panther Party and RAR Movement.

17   For an in-depth semiotic and sociological analysis of the language of fashion, seminal readings include, among many: Ronald Barthes's (1967) *Système de la mode*, and his essays on the topic, ranging from a socio-semiological analysis of clothing to a critical analysis of the meaning of gemstones and jewelry, the reenactment of traditional dichotomies between ancient and modern, and constant transformation through mixture of styles; Mary Douglas and Baron Isherwood's 1979 work, for their interpretation of consumerism as an information system; Daniel Roche's 1989 *La culture des apparences*, on the political, economic and socio-symbolic aspects of the material culture and its transformation from a status-oriented clothing selection to a style driven one.

southeastern Armenia to Aneda Zanetti's 2004 burkini - but also with words and phrases that become the language of politics.

There are metaphorical expressions that from everyday speech occasionally enter political language: one of these is the well-known proverb "God makes and apparel shapes", with the variants "Apparel makes the man" or "The tailor makes the man". As for many proverbs, it also admits its opposite version "clothes do not make the man", often used in political invectives, which is probably what Marx had in mind when he defined Louis-Napoleon Bonaparte as an "old crafty roué" who masqueraded knavery with grand costumes[18] and Winston Churchill implied when he disdainfully called Mahatma Gandhi a "half-naked fakir".[19] The same goes for the proverb "Good clothes make fine birds" and its alternative " Fine feathers make fine birds", whose opposite is inspired by a fable attributed to Aesop (The Jay and the Peacock), "it is not only fine feathers that make fine birds", and finds a similar message in the adage "You can't make a silk purse out of a sow's ear", meaning that it is impossible to transform poor quality items in successful products.[20] Other metaphors focus on the ability of fashion to disguise, hide, and finally reveal the truth, and this is exemplified by two turns of phrase: "To steal someone's clothes", recurring in British journalism, referring to a politician or political party presenting somebody else's ideas and policies as their own, and "to have something up in one's sleeve", which refers to using a secret idea or plan against an opponent. Both the expressions "to be all dressed up with nowhere to go", referring to being prepared for something which cannot be accomplished, and to do something "after a fashion", which implies it was not well done, allude to the transitory and idle aspect of fashion items.

On the other hand, there are metaphors originating in the political realm, which have then moved to everyday language. Take for instance "Big wig": since the 18th century the term has been used to indicate an important person or official. Referring humorously to British judges and barristers wearing wigs in courts, it is often used by reporters (also

---

18   Cfr. Karl Marx (1852).
19   Cfr. Peter Gonsalves (2009).
20   Proverbs and idioms here illustrated have been taken from the *Dictionary of Proverbs* (2000).

in the 70s' more popular version "biggies") to indicate important party members.[21] A similar reference to the formal attire of powerful white men, which has entered common usage, is "white gloves", meaning a person of high social or economic status, since white gloves for men were reserved for very formal occasions.[22] A similar but derogatory expression for the upper class is "silk stocking". Used by Jefferson against the wealthy Federalists and by Lincoln in reply to Colonel Richard Taylor who, despite being self-conceited and dandyish, tended to pose as a hard-working man, and to describe Whigs as aristocrats, it was also the name of the 7th Regiment of the New York Militia of the Union Army during the American Civil War. [23]

Some political expressions are a testimony of politicians' sassiness and wit or find their origin in anecdotes of their political history. "It takes the ragged boys to do the fighting" is a phrase attributed to Lincoln who, while staying in an inn in Boston, soon after the revolution, asked the hostess' daughter which soldiers she liked most. When the little girl replied that she liked the redcoats best, the President admitted that they looked better but their opponents, the patriots, although badly equipped, prevailed.[24] Lincoln is also credited with the word "bootblack", still used to diminish political opponents. He used it in reply to a foreign diplomat who was surprised at seeing him polishing his shoes. When the diplomat exclaimed: "What, Mr. President, you black your own boots?", Lincoln is reported to have replied. "Yes, whose do you black?".[25] Boot is indeed the object of many multi-words expressions used both in everyday language and in the political world: "get/give someone the boot", mostly used in passive constructions to indicate someone who has lost his/her job; "put the boot into someone or something" to indicate criticism levelled especially against a weak person

---

21   Cfr. Safire (2008), p. 54.
22   Over time, however, especially in non-political fields, the word has taken the different meaning of deferential behavior, being associated with the classic English butler's uniform. "Glove" has also inspired the idiom "take the gloves off" indicating somebody ready to fight or compete, also in politics. Cfr. *Collins Cobuild* (1995), p. 164.
23   Cfr. Safire (2008), pp. 660–661.
24   Cfr. Paul F. Boller, Jr. (1996), p. 16.
25   Ivi, p. 136.

or thing, "lick someone's boots" meaning to be obsequious or servile to someone powerful or influential, and "pull oneself up by one's boot-straps", indicating admiration for somebody who has improved his/her condition.[26]

Some other words reflect presidential character: the size of the hatband became, during Mckinley's presidency, a measurement of a politician's expanding ego, after a friend of his, Chicago editor H. H. Kohlsaat, told him after the inauguration that he was interested in knowing whether he would be able to wear the same hat after one-year adulation.[27] The expression, however, may well have been inspired by the phrase "Tight as Dick's hatband", indicating something absurd or perverse and deriving from Oliver Cromwell's son, Richard's unsuccess in wearing a crown.[28] Head covers and outer garments are the most productive of political metaphors. Some of these originate in the realm of campaign rhetoric, such as Carter's "spending cap", indicating a limit on allowed expenses, and later used during H.W. Bush's campaign for a second term and Bill Clinton's presidency, when the newly elected presidents bragged about keeping expenses below the spending cap approved by Congress.[29] Some others owe their existence to Presidential attire. Lincoln's habit of wearing a cap for most part of the day, like most people in old times, gave origin to the expression "keep something under one's hat", for keeping a secret; his "top hat", which he wore in war and peace and in formal and informal occasions, became a symbol of prestige and authority. His contemporaries defined his look "of unassuming simplicity", and on occasions even his coat was defined "shabby", but as his biographer Harold Holzer pointed out, his top hat would make him "look taller than any other man in the city", so that he couldn't be missed in a crowd.[30] Some one hundred and fifty years later, Donald Trump's MAGA hat, the "Make America Great Again" red cap, whose trademark he patented, and which was awarded the symbol of the year by the Stanford Symbolic Systems Program, has made history,

---

26   Cfr. *Colins Cobuild* (1995), pp. 43–44.
27   Cfr. Paul Boller (1996), p. 192.
28   Its first use in print is in the 1796 edition of Francis Grose's 1788 *Dictionary*.
29   Cfr. Safire (2008), p. 687.
30   Cfr. Stephen L. Carter (2013).

as much as it has been made by the "Pussy", pink, hand-made, knitted hat with ears, worn during the Women's March in Washington DC on January 21 as a form of protest to his inauguration and his 2005 "locker room" statement about grabbing women's genitals.[31]

Some other "hat" metaphors have different origins. The phrase "throw one's hat in the ring" to reveal one's intention to enter a political campaign or announce one's candidacy for an office or to try to win a contest is credited to Theodore Roosevelt who used it on his way to the Ohio Constitutional Convention in 1912 to reply to a reporter's question about whether he intended to run for president again. It derives from frontier boxing where a man ready to take on the challenge would toss his hat into the boxing ring, which was often set in the middle of bar-rooms by saloonkeepers to avoid brawls. Safire's *Dictionary* records examples of humorous variations of the construction: FDR's Interior secretary, Thomas E. Ickes, derided the 38-year-old Thomas E. Dewey, who announced his candidacy for President in 1940, by saying he had "tossed his diapers in the ring"[32], and in 1967, when Shirley Temple Black, the famous Hollywood child star, carved out a career in foreign affairs (she was appointed as US delegate to the UN by President Nixon), it was said she had thrown "her curls in the ring".[33] Frontier life and western movies have also inspired other hat metaphors: "all hat and no cattle" or also "big hat, no cattle", [34] meaning all talk but no action,

---

31 "Locker room talk" was the excuse used by Donald Trump during his second electoral debate on 9 October 2016 to explain his statement made years before during a conversation with the TV reporter Billy Bush, when he bragged: "when you're a star, they let you do it. You can do anything. Grab 'em by the pussy. You can do anything.". On the significance of "pussy hats", see Erin Reimel and Krystin Arneson (2017). Also read Johnson Hess (2017).

32 Also reported in the Sept. 15, 1941 edition of *Time*.

33 Cfr. Safire (2008), p. 310.

34 The earliest printed example of the expression is in *The Oklahoma News*, February 1937. In more recent times it was used by senator Robert Byrd in reference to Bush's Administration declaration of wanting to involve the UN in Iraq in 2003. Cfr. Hat Metaphors and Similes, Techfeatured, 9 August 2018, https://techfeatured.com.

deriving from the oversize hats used by cowboys in 1920s, and "black hats", meaning villains as opposed to "white hats", the good guys.[35]

Before fashion invented metallic, sheer, fishnet dresses and fire inspired textiles, politics coined the *Teflon-coated* president, an expression used by Representative Patricia Schroeder in 1983 to allude to Reagan's charm and wit which seemed to protect him from public displeasure and criticism no matter what he did and what dirt his opponents could uncover. The term and its derivate expression, "Teflonish", have been also used for Bill Clinton and Barack Obama, pinpointing a significant political phenomenon, the willingness of voters to excuse some politicians' shortcomings that they wouldn't accept in others lacking their charisma (Dickson 2013: 156). "Coat" and its compound words or derivational formations are quite frequent in political jargon: besides "coat holder", used since 1941 to indicate a political follower and then also somebody enjoying presidential trust and confidence, quite well-known expressions are "coattails" and the "coattail effect", deriving from the loose material on a jacket that hangs at the back below the waist. The first, indicating a man's formal jacket, was popularized by Congressman Lincoln in an 1848 speech in the House, referring to General Jackson's ability to attract and hold support, and later used in his presidential campaign to indicate straight-ticket voting;[36] the second is used in American politics to describe the impact an extremely popular or unpopular candidate has on other candidates in the same election. A popular candidate can help sweep other Election Day hopefuls into office. Meanwhile, an unpopular candidate can have the opposite effect, dashing the hopes of those running for offices lower down on the ballot. The expression has also entered nonpolitical contexts to

---

35   In 1977 it was used in connection to the Watergate scandal to distinguish good guys (wearing white hats in western movies) from bad guys (wearing black hats). Cfr. Safire (2008), p. 58 and 807.

36   See Campbell and Sumners (1990), for an explanation of the relation between a party's presidential vote in the states and its Senate vote, and Safire (2008: 132–3), for the origin of the expression. The author illustrates several cases of use of the metaphor, including Nixon's attack on Johnson's declining popularity referring to the clothing trends of the time: "There is a new fashion sweeping the country: skirts are shorter, pants are tighter and LBJ coattails are going out of style".

indicate someone benefiting from another's popularity. Equally famous
is the noun phrase "petticoat government", used to describe a local
government – usually a town council – in which all of the members
are female and which seems to have been first used by satirist Edward
Ward in the late 16th century to indicate an indirect rule by a woman.
It was used by Senator Albert Fall of New Mexico in reference to First
Lady Edith Wilson's assistance of her husband after he suffered from a
stroke in 1919. Although she claimed she was just carrying out the President's wishes, she acted in his place, hiding his true condition (speech
impairment and memory loss) even from the vice president and the
secretary of state until he recovered (Beyer 2007:148–149). The word
for the female undergarment was also used during Jackson's presidency
for the Eatons' affair. The president appointment of senator John Eaton
as his Secretary of War in 1831 was not welcomed by the ladies of
Washington, wives and sisters of the congressmen, scandalized by the
promiscuous past of Eaton's wife, a notable, flirtatious beauty, who was
then ostracized in social circles. Despite the President's defense of the
lady's reputation, the entire cabinet, including Eaton, had to resign for
what became known as the *Petticoat Affair* (Beyer 36–37).

   This discussion has no pretense of being exhaustive. Space lim-
its do not allow a lengthy description of all the fashion-related nouns
and adjectives used in the field of diplomacy, including "fashion diplomacy" or "closet diplomacy" for the habit of female political leaders and first ladies of wearing dresses with a symbolic meaning,[37]
"shirt-sleeve diplomacy"[38] for informal-speaking, plain international

---

37 For a lengthier discussion, read Benhke (2017) on "(Un)dressing the sovereign"
    (114–145).
38 The phrase appeared during McKinley's presidency, both in reference to
    his go-slow policy in the Spanish- Cuban crisis, which eventually led to the
    Spanish-American war in late 1897, and to his Secretary of State John Hay's
    straightforward Open Door Note to European countries' recommending trade
    on equal basis with China. In recent times, during Obama's Presidency, it was
    used to indicate informal face-to-face conversation between political leaders,
    conducted in absence of aides, secretaries, and staff members. The expression
    has a positive connotation due to the reference to hardworking implied by the
    related metaphor of "rolling up one's sleeves". Cfr. Safire (2008), p 655.

relations, and whose contrary is a "striped-pants diplomacy"[39], nor of metaphors related to color, such as "Alice Blue"[40], and "blue-ribbon panel",[41] to places such as "cloakroom",[42] "sons of basement",[43] "Guggi

---

39   "Striped pants", initially used as an adjective of diplomat, or civil servant, has become a substitute since the 2nd World War for the referent and also a reference to artificial formality. The expression may well have been originated from an anecdote involving FDR's presidency and Joseph P. Kennedy, the father of future president JFK. The President was thinking of giving him a position in his administration when his friend and supporter asked for the ambassadorship in England, an idea which intrigued the President, due to Joe Kennedy's Irish origin, but which puzzled him due to Joe's well-known bowlegs, which would make him look horrible and laughable in knee britches and silk stocking typically worn at the induction ceremony. It seems that he managed to convince the president when he obtained the British permission to wear a cutaway coat and striped pants. Cfr. Boller (1996), pp. 271–272.

40   "Alice blue" is a shade of cyan color by which became known the gowns worn by Theodore Roosevelt's daughter Alice, a beautiful, strong-willed and unconventional young lady who was also one of the most talked girls of her era, and which inspired the title of a song "Alice-blue gown", first performed by Edith Day at the Broadway musical Irene in 1919. Alice blue is also the color of the US Navy Insignia. Cfr. Dickson (2013), p. 21.

41   A blue-ribbon panel is a jury or commission, especially a government appointed committee, chosen for the expertise or integrity of its members. The compound adjective comes from the blue ribbon worn by members of the Order of the Garter, the most senior and exclusive British order of Chivalry and of the Order of the Holy Spirit in France, reserved to princes and nobles before the July Revolution. Cfr. Safire (2008), p. 66.

42   A "cloakroom", originally referring to the room where outer clothing, originally called "cloaks", was stored during one's stay, started to be used in the 1860s to indicate an anteroom in the Capitol building where senators and congressmen could meet to discuss privately and rest. In time, it acquired the negative connotation of a place where to bargain votes and gossip, becoming a synonym with rumor factory. Cfr. Safire (2008), p 129.

43   The expression is credited to Ronald Reagan. In March 1986, at the end of a rough press conference, the President referred to the journalists as "son of bitches". After a video recording of the event confirmed the use of the expletive, the reporters working in the basement offices of the White House started to wear T-shirts with the script "Sons of the Basement", until a few days later the President appeared wearing a yellow T-Shirt with the letters SOB on the front and the script "Save Our Budget" on the back. It seems that a *Time*'s journalist, Hugh Sidey, commented that he had not only SOB-ed but also defeated them. Cfr. Boller (1996), pp. 363–364.

gulch",[44] and to fabric production processes, such as "dyed-in-the-wool",[45] which equally originate in the political arena. Nor it is possible to indulge in the discussion of the structure and strategic function of these metaphors popularizing abstract concepts by using common lexicon, oftentimes conveying an implicit bias or an allusion to that lack of transparency which politicians and politics are all too often accused of.[46] Likewise, it is beyond the scope of this paper to discuss the obvious connection between fashion and political image and the importance of garment selection for a politician's career. Presidential candidates' and incumbents' fashion choices have often affected their success: John F. Kennedy's preference for formal dresses to disguise his young age, Richard Nixon's makeup failure in the first televised debate against the handsome and tanned young Democratic senator in 1960, and Eugene McCarthy's "Clean for Gene" campaign in 1968 are well known examples.[47]

---

44   "Gucci Gulch" is an alliterative construction which repeats the Gucci logo, GG, to indicate the corridors outside the hearing room of the United States Senate Committee on Ways and Means or the Senate Finance Committee, where lobbyists usually wait for political decisions. It mocks their highly paid jobs by hinting at their wearing expensive Italian suits and shoes. Cfr. Barrett (2006), p. 125.

45   Dyed-in-the-wool, which comes from textile coloring procedure, consisting in dying the wool before it is spun into threads, so that the color lasts longer, is used as an adjective for a firm, opinioned, inveterate person and for party members (mostly Democrats) who are proud of their party label. Cfr. Safire (2008), p. 202.

46   On the cognitive function of metaphors, see George Lakoff and Mark Johnson's 1980 seminal work and Elena Semino's 2008 analysis of metaphors in discourse, highlighting the effects of source-domain choices on the representation of the target domain; for an analysis of the most frequent metaphors in political argumentation, see Jonathan Charteris-Black (2005), who, however, does not explore clothing ones.

47   Senator Eugene (Gene) McCarthy challenged the incumbent president Lyndon Johnson on an anti-Vietnam War platform. While hoping of getting the support of young activists, he also tried to keep the favor of political moderates distancing himself from "hippie" youths. In order to do so, his campaign set a strict dress and grooming code for volunteers, which implied haircuts for many long-haired Left sympathizers, transformed overnight in the reassuring kid next door. See Hillman (2015: XIII–XV) and Howard Husock's 2007 commentary. On the Kennedy-Nixon debate, which changed political communication modality, see Beyer (2007:176–179) and Auer (1962), among many.

Fashion and politics have always been related. Not only do political choices impact garment production systems and buyers' spending but they also respond to fashion trends which permeate cultural boundaries and linguistic habits. From Versailles court's *talon rouge* (red heel) signifying elegance and political privilege and 18th century parliamentary *whip* indicating a person who is appointed by a political party to act as a liaison between the leaders and the other members of the party to Ronald Reagan's "little old ladies in tennis shoes",[48] Clinton's "zipper problem",[49] and George W. Bush's "women of cover",[50] fashion-related political jargon confirms that clothing is entangled with power and that politics as fashion is a commodified art, producing some volatile, short-lived phenomena (including linguistic turns) and some long-lasting results such as accepted neologisms and idioms which, like functional and necessary clothing items, survive despite their evolution in shape and fabric. Ultimately, the body politic is a dressed body in distinctive spaces and times.

---

48 *Little old ladies in tennis shoes,* to define female right-wing extremists, was first used to attack Senator Barry Goldwater's supporters during his campaign for the Republican nomination in 1963, being some of them resolute, unsophisticated elderly women. Pinpointing the sexism and ageism in the expression, Ronald Reagan frequently used it to his own advantage to address his audience during his campaign for Governor of California in 1966. Cfr. Safire (2008), pp. 395–396.

49 A *zipper problem,* rather than describing the occasional jamming of a zipper, is a metaphor for loose morals of a candidate who is accused of marital infidelity. It refers to Bill Clinton-Monica Lewinsky scandal and his being re-elected despite that. Cfr. Safire (2008), p. 828.

50 It was coined by George W. Bush in 2001 and used on several occasion to mention Muslim women by referring to their religion-prescribed headscarves. Cfr. Dickson (2013), p. 173.

References

Andrews, Jonathan. 2007a. The (Un)dress of the Mad Poor in England, c.1650–1850, part 1. *History of Psychiatry* 18(1): 5–24.

Andrews, Jonathan. 2007b. The (Un)dress of the Mad Poor in England, c.1650–1850', part 2. *History of Psychiatry* 18(2): 131–56.

Auer, Jeffrey J. 1962. The counterfeit debates. In Sidney Kraus (ed.), *The Great Debates: Kennedy vs Nixon*, 142–149. Bloomington, IN: Indiana University Press.

Barret, Grant (Ed.). 2006. *The Oxford Dictionary of American Political Slang*. Oxford, and New York: Oxford University Press.

Barthes, Ronald. 1967. *Système de la mode*. Paris: Éd. du Seuil.

Bartlett, Djurdja (Ed.). 2019. *Fashion and Politics*. New Haven, and London: Yale University Press.

Benhke, Andreas. 2017. The International Politics of Fashion. Being Fab in a Dangerous World. London, and New York: Routledge.

Beyer, Rick. 2007. *The Greatest Presidential Stories Never Told: 100 tales from history to astonish, bewilder & stupefy*. New York: Collins.

Boller, Paul F. Jr. 1996. *Presidential Anecdotes*. Oxford: Oxford University Press.

Campbell, James E. and Joe Sumners. 1990. Presidential Coattails in Senate Elections. *The American Political Science Review* 84(2): 513–524.

Carter, Stephen L. 2013. *Abraham Lincoln's Top Hat: The Inside Story*. Available at the site: Abraham Lincoln's Top Hat: The Inside Story | History| Smithsonian Magazine. Washington, D.C.: Smithsonian Institution.

Charteris-Black, Jonathan. 2005. *Politicians and Rhetoric. The Persuasive Power of Metaphor*. New York: Palgrave Macmillan.

Sinclair, John. 1995. *Colins Cobuild Dictionary of Idioms*. 1995. London: Harpers Collins.

Conoly, John. 1846. Lectures on the construction and government of lunatic asylums. *The Lancet* 48(1198): 167–170.

Dickson, Paul. 2013. *Words from the White House*. New York: Walker & Company.

Law, Jonathan (ed.). 2000. *Dictionary of Proverbs*. London: Penguin Books.

Douglas, Mary and Baron Isherwood. 1979. *The World of Goods*. New York: Basic Books.

DuPlessis, Robert S. 2012. What did slaves wear? Textile regimes in the French Caribbean. *Monde(s)* 1(1): 175–191.

Earle, Rebecca. 2019. Race, clothing and identity: Sumptuary laws. In Giorgio Riello and Unlika Rublack (eds.), *The Right to Dress: Sumptuary Laws in a Global Perspective*, c.1200–1800. Cambridge: Cambridge University Press, 325–345.

Eskridge, William N. 1999. *Gaylaw: Challenging the Apartheid of the Closet*. Cambridge, Mass.: Harvard University Press.

Gaugele, Ekle and Monica Titton (Eds.). 2019. Fashion as politics: Dressing dissent. *Fashion Theory*, special issue, 23(6): 65–756.

Gonsalves, Peter. 2009. 'Half-Naked Fakir', The story of Gandhi's personal search for sartorial integrity. *Gandhi Marg* 31(1). New Delhi: Gandhi Peace Foundation, 5–30.

Gonsalves, Peter. 2009. Half naked fakir. The story of Gandhi's personal search for sartorial integrity. *Gandhi Marg* 31(1). https://www.mkgandhi.org/articles/half-naked-fakir.html [accessed 15 March 2022].

Grose, Francis. 1788. *Dictionary of the Vulgar Tongue*. London: S. Hooper. https://publicdomainreview.org/collection/a-classical-dictionary-of-the-vulgar-tongue-1788 [accessed 14 March 2022].

Hamlett, Jane and Lesley Hoskins. 2013. Comfort in small things? Clothing, control and agency in county lunatic asylums in nineteenth and early twentieth century England. *Journal of Victorian Culture* 18, 1(1): 93–114.

Haulman, Kate. 2011. *The Politics of Fashion in Eighteenth-Century America. Gender and American Culture*. Chapel Hill: The University of North Carolina Press.

Hebdige, Dick. 1979. *Subculture. The Meaning of Style*. London: Methuen & Co.

Hess, Johnson. 2017. Trump caps and 'pussy hats': Here's who benefits when your purchase is political. https://www.cnbc.com/2017/02/07/trump-caps-and-pink-hats-who-benefits-when-your-purchase-is-political.html [accessed 12 March 2022]

Hide, Louise. 2014. *Gender and Class in English Asylums, 1890–1914*. New York: Palgrave Macmillan.

Hillman, Betty L. 2015. *Dressing for the Culture Wars. Style and Politics of Self-presentation in the 1960s and 1970s*. Lincoln, and London: University of Nebraska Press.

Husock, Howard. 2007. Clean for Gene. *The New York Sun*. https://www.manhattan-institute.org/html/clean-gene-1302.html [accessed 9 March 2022]

Iwaszko, Tadeuz. 2000. "The housing, clothing and feeding of the prisoners". In Waclaw Długoborski and Franciszek Piper (eds.), *Auschwitz 1940–1945, Central Issues in the History of the Camp*, vol. II: "The Prisoners – Their Life and Work". Oświęcim: Auschwitz-Birkenau State Museum, 51–63.

Lakoff, George and Mark Johnson. 1980. *Metaphors We Live by*. Chicago: The University of Chicago Press.

Lemire, Beverly. 2020. "Shirts and snowshoes: Imperial agendas and Indigenous agency in globalizing North America". In Beverly Lemire and Giorgio Riello (eds.), *Dressing the Global Bodies. The Political Power of Dress in the World*. London, and New York: Routledge, 65–84.

Marchetti, Maria C. 2020. *Moda e politica. La rappresentazione simbolica del potere*. Milano: Meltemi Press.

Marx, Karl. 1852. *The Eighteenth Brumaire of Louis Bonaparte III*. https://www.marxists.org/archive/marx/works/1852/18th-brumaire/ch05.htm [accessed 9 March 2022].

Mayer, Tara. 2020. Dressing apart. Indian elites and the politics of fashion in British India, c. 1750–1850. In Beverly Lemire and Giorgio Riello (eds.), *Dressing the Global Bodies. The Political Power of Dress in the World*. London, and New York: Routledge, 225–239.

Norris, Herbert. 1998. *Medieval Costume and Fashion*. New York: Dover Publications, a reprint of a 1927 publication by Dent & Sons, London.

Piponnier, Francoise and Perrine Mane. 1997. *Dress in the Middle Ages*. New Haven: Yale University Press.

Polhemus, Ted. 1994. *Streetsyle. From Sidewalk to Catwalk*. London: Thames & Hudson.

Reimel, Erin and Krystin Arneson. 2017. Here's the powerful story behind the pussyhats at the women's march. Beyond empowering.

https://www.glamour.com/story/the-story-behind-the-pussyhats-at-the-womens-march. [accessed 12 March 2022].

Richmond, Vivienne. 2013. *Clothing the Poor in Nineteenth-century England*. Cambridge: Cambridge University Press.

Riello, Giorgio. 2020. Fashion in the four parts of the world. In Beverly Lemire and Giorgio Riello (eds.), *Dressing Global Bodies, The Political Power of Dress in World History*. London, New York: Routledge, 41– 64.

Roche, Daniel. 1989. *La culture des apparences. Une histoire du vêtement* (XVII- XVIII siècle). Mesnil-sur-l'Estrée: Fayard

Safire, William. 2008. *Safire's Political Dictionary*. Oxford, and New York: Oxford University Press.

Saller, Richard P. 1998. "Symbols of gender and status hierarchies in the Roman household". In Sandra R. Joshel and Sheila Murghan (eds.), *Women and Slaves in Greco-Roman Culture. Differential Equations*. New York: Routledge, 85–91.

Saunders, Richard. 1782. On Dress. *In Poor Richard Improved: Being an Almanack and Ephemeris for the Year of Our Lord*. Philadelphia: B. Franklin and D. Hall.

Sears, Clare. 2015. *Cross-dressing, Law, and Fascination in Nineteenth-Century San Francisco*. Durham and London: Duke University.

Semino, Elena. 2008. *Metaphor in Discourse*. Cambridge: Cambridge university Press.

Suderland, Maya. 2013. *Inside Concentration Camps. Social Life at the Extremes*. Cambridge: Polity Press.

Sugiura, Miki. 2020. Garments in circulation. The economies of slave clothing in the eighteenth-century Dutch Cape Colony. In Beverly Lemire and Giorgio Riello (eds.), *Dressing the Global Bodies. The Political Power of Dress in the World*. London, and New York: Routledge, 104–130.

Theune, Claudia. 2018. Clothes as expression of action in former concentration camps. *International Journal of Historical Archeology* 22: 492–510.

Tranberg Hansen, Karen. 2010. The city, clothing consumption and the search for 'the latest' in colonial and postcolonial Zambia. In Beverly Lemire (ed.), *The Force of Fashion in Politics and Society*. London, and New York: Routledge, 213–234.

Turner, Terence. 2012. The social skin. *HAU: Journal of Ethnographic Theory* 2(2): 486–504.

White, Sophie. 2020. Dressing enslaved Africans in colonial Lousiana. In Beverly Lemire and Giorgio Riello (eds.), *Dressing the Global Bodies. The Political Power of Dress in the World*. London, and New York: Routledge, 85–103.

Stefania Biscetti

"It's never 'just a *trouser!*'": Bipartite Garment Nouns as Singulars in the Language of Fashion

1. Introduction

This article explores the use of bipartite nouns as singulars in the language of fashion. Bipartite nouns (e.g., *trousers, pants, leggings*) denote "articles of dress consisting of two equal parts which are joined together" (Quirk et al. 1985: § 5.76). They are a semantic subcategory of *pluralia tantum* nouns, which, it is said, occur only in the plural. It is also said of bipartites that they do not "satisfy the test for count nouns" (i.e., they cannot occur with cardinal numbers, e.g.,?two *jeans*; Payne & Huddleston 2002: 342), that they are emblematic of "the non-arbitrariness of the relationship between grammatical form and meaning" (Wierzbicka 1988: 514–515; Wisniewsky 2010: 181–182), and that they can be used as singulars only to refer to the type, model or style of garments, not to individual items (Wickens 1992).

Using evidence from *The Vogue Archive* (America), where the form *trouser* occurs 803 times with singular verb agreement (e.g., ... a boyfriend-cut *trouser* <u>makes</u> for the perfect cheering ensemble (Vogue 205/2 (Feb 1, 2015): 170)) across a time span of 129 years, this paper wants to challenge these claims about a class of nouns whose use as singulars is emblematic of - but not unique to - the technical language of fashion experts.

2. Bipartite nouns in the literature

The general contention among grammarians is that bipartite garment nouns exist only in the plural, that the singular form (e.g., *one/*

a trouser) is either ungrammatical or proper to colloquial language (Quirk et al. 1985: § 5.76) or, alternatively, that it is restricted to the specialized "language of commerce" and clothing. "The crucial feature of this usage is that the reference is to types, not individual specimens" (Payne & Huddleston 2002: 342). Thus, bipartites are essentially uncountable.

Quirk et al. (1985: § 5.76) observe that summation plurals (as bipartites are also called) require plural pronoun and plural verb concord (e.g., I like these trousers/this pair of trousers. How much are they?), even when they are preceded by "pair". Yet, they "differ from ordinary plural nouns in that they are not generically thought of as denoting plural number", i.e., they are thought of as referring to one item only.[1] Hence the need to express the semantic opposition singular vs plural with the classifier "pair(s) of". The fact that bipartite garment nouns are "notionally singular, though morphologically and syntactically plural" (Quirk et al. 1985: § 10.43, Note [c]) would seem to explain the "occasional" and colloquial uses of the singular form of the verb (in utterances like "?*Is my scissors on the table?") and of the indefinite article "a" (as in (?) a *scissors*) with these nouns, uses considered unacceptable in formal English. Also the use of cardinal numbers with bipartites (?two trousers) is considered informal and barely acceptable in formal contexts.

Payne & Huddleston (2002: 341) have a different view on the form-meaning relation of bipartite garment nouns, whose plural form and occurrence with "pair" is said to be motivated by the bipartite structure of the objects they denote. Yet, "outside the *pair* construction, bipartite plurals characteristically apply to single garments . . .". This is why few speakers would find "?I've only got two jeans" acceptable, which means that "bipartite plurals cannot be said to satisfy the test for count nouns." (Payne & Huddleston 2002: 342).

Scholars are divided on the notional singularity of bipartites. Gleason (1961: 24) (quoted in Wierzbicka 1991: 375) could not find any semantic justification for the plural form of words like *trousers, shorts,*

---

1   Carther & McCarthy (2006: 343) point out that referential ambiguity may sometimes arise, as in "I didn't buy much but I did buy some *trousers*", where "one pair or several could be indicated".

slacks, and *pants,* which, he claimed, are plural only "by a convention" because the object they name is one single item. Likewise, Williams (1994: 13) considers "pants" an "'arbitrary' plural" the formal idiomaticity of which is due to the meaning "something worn on the legs in such and such a way" and is extended to all nouns that have this meaning (e.g., *jeans, shorts, cut-offs,* etc.). Nenonen & Niemi's (2010) experiment on the degree of isomorphy between grammatical number and conceptual numerosity in Finnish nouns provides ambiguous evidence for the notional singularity of *pluralia tantum,* represented by the word *vankkuri-t* 'wagon-pl' in the experiment. This lexical item was thought by participants as representing "one" referent in 305 out of 476 responses, and "many" referents in 171 responses (i.e., in 35 % of the total). Yet, the authors conclude that "the plurale tantum words, when presented as isolated items, are relatively biased towards MANY" (Nenonen & Niemi 2010: 120).

To the notional singularity of all bipartites, Corbett (2019: 54) objects that *scissors* is not necessarily singular in meaning, because it can denote more than one item, as in "All these scissors are blunt". In other words, the semantics of *scissors* would be that of a countable noun. The same holds for *pants,* which occurs exactly in the same syntactic environment in my data ("all these *pants* at The San Francisco New World Clothing Trust", Vol. 156/Issue 3 (Aug 15, 1970): 88). In fact, Corbett (2019: 63) considers *trousers* countable, although he does not go deeper into the question.

Cognitive scientists such as Nickels et al. (2015: 293) say that "the concept SCISSORS can conceptually refer to a single or multiple entity"; while for Langacker (1987:47) "the assumption that they [*scissors, pants,* etc.] are semantically singular is incorrect" because their morphological and syntactic plurality "reflects conventional imagery" and highlights "the bipartite character of the objects named". It is worth noting, however, that Langacker is not implying a motivated relation between grammatical number and conceptual numerosity. For him, the fact that bipartites are "plural in form (and largely in behaviour)" is "a matter of convention (not cognitive necessity)" (Langacker 1987:47).

Wierzbicka (1988: 515) strongly believes that nouns designating dual objects "which have two identical parts fulfilling the same function within the whole" are non-arbitrary *pluralia tantum*. She claims that the "non-existence" of the singular form "*one trouser was torn" to refer to one trouser leg and the co-occurrence of these nouns with the classifier "pair of" reflect the fact that the two symmetrical parts of the dual garment "are not thought of as separate entities" and therefore cannot be counted singularly (unlike the members of paired but separate entities such as "gloves", "socks", etc.). This view is in line with the Cognitive Individuation Hypothesis (Wisniewski 2009: 167), which holds that "there is a conceptual basis for the count—mass noun distinction". Since the two parts of dual objects are not discrete, separate, and independent entities, it is not possible to count them or refer to them individually, and therefore the nouns that name these objects are uncountable, and only plural.

To this view, Corbett objects that if the relation between form and meaning were indeed a natural one, bipartites should be encoded as *dualia tantum* in languages that have dual number. What we find, instead, is that "in Slovene, which has a singular-dual-plural system" nouns like *trousers* "are pluralia tantum and not dualia tantum" (Corbett 2019: 85). Chierchia (1998:57) is also critical about iconicity between word grammar and the ontological nature of their referents and concludes "while the mass/count distinction is not altogether indifferent to how things are inherently structured, it appears to be independent of it, which is what makes such a distinction a strictly grammatical one".

Countability is extensively discussed by Allan (1980), who sees it as a gradable property of nouns. Allan identifies a set of criteria to establish the degree of countability of English nouns and concludes that nouns like *trousers, braces/suspenders, pants* and *tights*, are "regular" *pluralia tantum* sharing the same countability characteristics as *scissors* (e.g., which cannot occur with quantifiers such as *one/a/an, each, every, many, a few*) and having "referents perceived as two moveable leg-like members pinioned to a bridge at one end, or so as to cross each other." (Allan 1980: 559) The connection between semantics and the countability profile of *scissors* is intentionally not made clear, because the author focuses on the syntactic environment of nouns. Of the singular form, it is only said that it is the "base", uncountable form of these nouns (e.g., *suspender*) and that it occurs when they are used adjectivally (e.g., *suspender* belt) (Allan 1980: 554). We shall see (par. 4) that

Allan's countability tests have given different results for *trousers* in our data.[2]

Wickens (1992) sees number as both a grammatical and semantic category and provides the most thorough description of the various uses "in contemporary English of the zero version, e.g., *trouser*" (Wickens 1992: 99), thus countering what Mencken (1963: 558) could write about thirty years before on the use of the singular (i.e., as belonging "to the argot of men's tailors and clothing salesmen"). According to Wickens (1992: 121), the plural form of "bifurcate garment names" is cognitively motivated by "the experience of the functional alternance or opposition of the two halves or legs which seem to move in opposite directions and . . . occupy separate spaces" and is always used with a "narrow and concrete individual sense" (p. 126).

The singular form, instead, expresses at least three main types of generic, nonindividual senses:

a) the "species sense", which refers to "a style, type, model, brand or the like" (e.g., "a modified 'peg-top' trouser [.].was revived"; "the seersucker is the famous Shaped Trouser") (pp. 123–124);

b) the "generic sense", which is even more abstract and distanced form an individual specimen than the "species sense" (e.g., "what is a Jean?"; "The Trouser throughout history", p. 128);

c) the "mass" noun sense (e.g., "All the rest was mustache, pelisse and calico trouser"; The dog had a bit of trouser in his mouth, p. 131);

d) other senses, which may evoke "all the parts of a [generic] whole" (e.g., . . . is sewn-in to every Jaymar pant sold in Canada); may express a "subset of the garment" (e.g., "The businessman will wear . . . a jean with mix'n match western jacket").

With these considerations in mind, I am going to reconsider the issue of countability of bipartite garment nouns in fashion discourse using Allan's (1980) countability tests, challenge the *pluralia tantum* status of bipartite nouns, see whether the singular can only be used to refer to types and not to single specimens, and suggest a cognitive and

---

2   Allan does not acknowledge any database for his investigation, which is therefore assumed to rely on the writer's own intuition as a native speaker of English.

experientially based account for singular usage. But before proceeding, a description of the database is in order.

3. The database

The Vogue Archive contains the entire run of *Vogue* magazine (US edition) from the first issue (December 17th, 1892) to the latest issue (current month). The magazine was a weekly publication[3] until February 12th, 1910. Then, from February 15th, 1910, it was turned into a fortnightly publication[4] by Condé Nast, who had bought it the year before. Vogue continued to be issued twice a month until December 1972, and from January 1973 it became the monthly publication that we know today. The number of issues published per year has not been steady through time, especially between 1943 and 1948, when it was reduced from 24 to 20 issues.

The present research is based on a total number of 2,941 issues (spanning from the first 1892 issue to the December 2021 issue) "reproduced in high-resolution color page images". This means that the Archive is designed to look for images, not text, and that a word count or even an approximate estimate of its size is not possible. This also means that the Archive does not make an easy corpus to interrogate for the linguist. Search results are not given with the key word in context. For each search result the user must open the corresponding document (which may consist of one or several pages) and look for the search word manually. This operation is facilitated by the search word being highlighted in light blue, but this helping tool/facility is not always working (i.e., the keyword is either not highlighted or it is mistaken for some other word), therefore corpus querying can be very time consuming.

---

3   *Vogue* was issued weekly on Saturdays (from December 17th, 1892, to September 16th, 1893); then it was issued on Thursdays (Sep 21st, 1893 - September 18th, 1909) and then again on Saturdays (September 25th, 1909 - February 12th, 1910).
4   From February 15th, 1910, to November 15th, 1972, it was published "on the first and fifteenth of every month" (*Vogue*, Feb 15th, 1910: 15).

The only contents that appear in text format are the captions to images or photographs, for which the database is designed. Another major drawback of the *Vogue Archive* is that the results of a query do not correspond in number to the actual occurrences (token frequency) of the search word, but to the number of documents (e.g., advertisement, table of contents, cover, feature, etc.) where the keyword occurs, and this may occur more than once in the same document.

The lexical item chosen to represent the class of bipartite garment nouns denoting items of clothing is *trouser(s)*,[5] which occurs 803 times in the singular and 5,787 times in the plural. Although frequency counts are not possible, the 803 occurrences of *trouser* are remarkable in number when compared with the 1,500 examples[6] collected by Wickens (1992) and may already suggest that *trousers* should be reconsidered as "plural dominant" (Baayen et al. 1997) rather than "plural only" in this discourse domain, at least.

4. *Trousers* and countability

In this section I am going to put *trouser(s)* (and *pant(s)*) to Allan's (1980) tests for countability to establish its degree of countability and thus verify its status as a *plurale tantum* noun. A noun is countable if it can occur with "any quantifier which necessarily identifies one or more discrete entities" (Allan 1980: 541) or a numeral. Such quantifiers are called "denumerators", and include *one, a(n), each, every, either, three, several, many, both, (a) few*. By contrast, "*no, all* and *some*

---

5   The reason for not choosing *pant(s)* (which is in fact a lot more frequent than *trouser(s)*) is that there is a considerable gap between the "raw" search results and the number of relevant occurrences. To give an idea, *pant* occurs 18 times and *pants* 65 times in the time span 1892–1902, but the actual results are 1 and 18 respectively (e.g., *pant*-suit; "gents' *pants*"). In most cases the software has mistaken items like "pant o' mine", "company", "panting", "rampant", "Paris", "participant", "occupant", "flippant" for the search word. *Pants* will be only considered for the countability tests.

6   These examples were provided by "at least fifty" nouns (both singular and plural) denoting a bifurcate garment in present-day English (Wickens 1992: 123).

do not necessarily denumerate". (Allan 1980: 542) Unlike countable nouns, "pluralia tantum nouns are countable only with fuzzy denumerators ... which do not state a precise number" (p. 548–549) such as *(a) few, several, many, a dozen or so, about fifty*, and high round numbers (e.g., *four hundred, fifty thousand*). The noun *scissors* fails the countability test with a unit quantifier (i.e. a(n)/one + N) (**a/one scissors*) and its acceptability with a fuzzy plural quantifier is dubious (*?How many scissors;?Quite a few scissors*). Let us now apply the two tests to *trouser(s)* and *pant(s)*.

- "Test with a unit quantifier (A + N Test)".

As expected, search for the phrases "*a/one trousers*" yielded zero results, due to its colloquial, informal register. Also, no occurrence was found of "*each/either/several/both trouser(s)*". However, what I did find was one occurrence of *one trouser* (1); 4 occurrences of *trousers/pants* with a numeral (2–5); and one occurrence of *every trouser* (6):

(1) He created two short skirts (one in silk crepe, the other in lace), *one trouser* (silk crepe), and one slip dress (silk crepe). The silk crepe skirt and pants lend themselves equally to travelling, business appointments, or "lighthearted evenings." (Vogue 181/6 (Jun 1, 1991): 140).

(2) There are seven jacket options (from boyish and drapey – mine – to cropped and precise); *six trousers* (from skinny to wide-leg); one straight skirt; and a nifty vest. (Vogue 200/9 (Sep 1, 2012): 486, 488).

(3) In the past decade, *two pants* above all have made our backsides look shapely and our legs longer: The Seven jean and the Katayone Adeli low-rise flat front trouser ... (Vogue 196/11 (Nov 1, 2006): 196).

(4) After Spaniel has perfected the silhouettes (25 to 30 jackets a season, about fifteen dresses, *five to ten pants*, ten to fifteen skirts), she decides which fabrics to use for each one. (Vogue 185/5, (May 1, 1995): 138).

(5) Three pairs day shoes at $7.50 ... 22.50. One pair mules ... 3.95. Six pairs gloves (...) ... 12.00. *Six pants* (...) at $2.95. (Vogue 89/2 (Jan 15, 1937): 115).

(6) ... and with every skirt, *every trouser* you own, no matter what texture, what color, what time or place. (Vogue 166/8 (Aug 1, 1976): 115).

These results are enough to say that, unlike *scissors* (Allan 1980: 549), *trousers* does not fail the A + N Test for countability. What increases the degree of countability of this bipartite noun and tells us that it is fully countable are the 13 occurrences where *a trouser*[7] is used to denote one leg of a pair of trousers (7–9) or the whole garment (10–15)

(7) So far the popular English demi-saison costume seems to be a morning coat of vicuna or rough cloth, a brown linen waistcoat buttoned high, and *a trouser* with a plain stripe in it on a dark ground. (Vogue 6/12 (Sep 19, 1895): 182).

(8) The new *robe d'intérieur* at the lower right settles the matter by affecting a compromise. A "trouser" robe, this, with *a trouser* for one leg only, and a skirt all to itself for the other leg. (Vogue 49/7 (Apr 1, 1917): 78).

(9) Fashion editors ... had problems with bracelets made of cat-food cans and suits with *a trouser* on one leg and a skirt on the other. (Vogue 181/3 (Mar 1, 1991): 397).

(10) [Empire bicycle skirt] The skirt combines the comfort and convenience of *a trouser*, with the grace and beauty of a round skirt. (Vogue 9/16 (Apr 22, 1897): xxvi).

(11) ... but what if the poor lady be forced to wear a skirt which resembles *a trouser*? (Vogue 40/6 (Sep 15, 1912): 84).

(12) Best has shorts-and-skirt suits of cotton crepe that are exceptionally well cut (a most important feature when the hang of *a trouser* makes all the difference between grace and ungainliness). (Vogue 75/6 (Mar 15, 1930): 140).

(13) ... thinness also has to do with finish – the thinness of a waistband on a skirt, on *a trouser*, the edging at the neck of a T-shirt. (Vogue 166/5 (May 1, 1976): 133).

(14) On trousers of lighter weight, fabric cuffs make less sense: they give the pants legs a little more weight, keep them from riding up. But cuffs make less sense on *a trouser* that has weight and body – or, say, on a golf trouser, where cuffs would just be sand catchers. (Vogue 168/8 (Aug 1, 1978): 250).

(15) The classic finish – classic style – of *a trouser* in flannel or gabardine (...). (Vogue 169/10 (Nov 1, 1979): 313).

(16) Whether you want to feel androgynous and sort of rangy in *a trouser* and a shirt, or very, very romantic in a soft, full skirt at night, ... (Vogue 182/5 (May 1, 1992): 263).

(17) "To me, *a trouser* with a man's cut is still the most elegant thing a woman can wear," says Armani (Vogue 182/8 (Aug 1, 1992): 271).

(18) ... the three-piece suit has undergone a thorough transformation, ... and offering either *a trouser* or skirt to go with the jacket, ... (Vogue 200/9 (Sep 1, 2010): 485).

---

7   The phrase "*a trouser*" was found to occur another 44 times with *trouser* used as noun modifier, e.g., a *trouser*-skirt; a *trouser* leg; a *trouser* petticoat, a *trouser* material, a *trouser* crease, a *trouser* pocket.

(19) At Céline, *a trouser* with leather-stripe details is pronounced "the most perfect pant ever made!" (Vogue 201/8 (Aug 1, 2011): 121).

- "Test with a fuzzy (plural) denumerator (F + Ns Test)".

Let us now see if *trousers* may combine with quantifiers which "unambiguously define(s) countables" (Allan 1980: 550). No occurrence with *several, about + numeral, a dozen or so* was found in the database. However, I could find 5 occurrences of *many trousers* (20–23) and one occurrence of *few pants* (24), which tell us that *trousers* does not fail the (F + Ns Test) either:

(20) "Seems to me you buy a great *many trousers*, Alfred. I notice you have on another new pair to-day." (Vogue 1/22 (May 13, 1893): 306).

(21) *Many trousers* are now made with small straps and buckles on the sides of the band, just above the hips ... (Vogue 25/11 (Mar 16, 1905): 374).

(22) *Many trousers* are made without this buckle .... (Vogue 19/7 (Feb 13, 1902): 125).

(23) The white flannel trousers to be seen in this shop deserve several encomiums, too. Unlike *many trousers*, they make you look divinely hipless, ... (Vogue 77/7 (Apr 1, 1931): 102).

(24) What else are stores stocking up on? One informal survey found suits, special blouses, and skirts – skirts, everywhere. Very *few pants*. (Vogue 169/7 (Aug 1, 1979): 186).

These results mean that *trouser(s)* (and virtually other nouns denoting bifurcated items of clothing "worn on the legs" (Williams 1994: 13)) are not "regular" *pluralia tantum* nouns but form a set of "plural dominant" nouns.

5. *Trouser*: Types of reference

In this section I am going to look at the types of meanings expressed by the singular form *trouser* in the data base, more precisely, I am going to see if *trouser* can only be used with generic reference to style, model, brand or type (Wickens's (1992) "species sense") and to any piece of clothing worn on the legs (Wickens's "generic sense"), or if it can be used to refer to single specimens as well.

With only few exceptions, the singular was found to express either a species sense (25–29) or a generic sense (30–33):[8]

(25) I own tons of Balenciaga: the turquoise tote, a black tuxedo jacket, the brown suede hobo bag from two years ago, and *the trouser* with gold piping for spring. (Vogue 195/4 (Apr 1, 2005): 166).

(26) *The petti-trouser*, a new substitute for the half-slip, goes down to the knee, smoothly, trimly; slipping snugly under close-hauled clothes—lined suits and dresses, for instance, or slacks (Vogue 132/2 (Aug 1, 1958): 127).

(27) Instead of the flared or full pants, they [the French] take to *the trouser* that falls in a dead-straight line from the waistband. (Vogue 162/1 (Jul 1, 1973): 84).

(28) ... he [George Brummel] saw the decline and fall of knee breeches for common wear, and *the trouser* invented by himself, take their place; (Vogue 35/6 (Feb 5, 1910): 5).

(29) The no-fuss neutrality of a cardi-jacket, *a slouchy trouser*, and color-blocked brogues make way for a bold approach to casual dressing—perfect for taking in a screening or two at New York's Tribeca Film Festival. (Vogue 204/4 Apr 1, 2014: 270).

(30) *The trouser*, the tunic, and the set-in sleeve were features of the earliest garments recorded in the North, ... (Vogue 59/3 (Feb 1, 1922): 54).

(31) I like it when *the trouser* breaks on the shoe. (Vogue 187/8 (Aug 1, 1997): 181).

(32) In order to remove any one pair, the particular rod over which it is hung is simply pulled out of the rack at the side and *the trouser* released. (Vogue 17/3 (Jan 17, 1901): 46, 47).

(33) But in the West (...) *Vir* has made *the trouser* his prerogative, ... (Vogue 109/2 (Jan 15, 1947): 86).

No instance of "mass" noun effect (Wickens 1992) was found. Reference to individual specimens has been found where *trouser* collocates with the demonstrative "this" (28), and possibly when *trouser* occurs in captions to photographs/images, where the text-image interaction triggers an indexical function of the bipartite noun, as in (29–31):

(34) "I love *this* superwide *trouser* with a sexy drapey Rick Owens tank and cropped jacket." (Vogue 198/6, (Jun 1, 2008): 92).

(35) [Advertisement] The caftan, about $78. The tunic, about $78. And *the trouser*, $42. (Vogue 166/2 (Feb 1, 1976): 52).

---

8   The "species sense" is also expressed in (9), (14), (17), (19), and the "generic sense" in (12), (13), (16), (18).

(36) [Advertisement] His [Ralph Lauren] silk pleated dinner trouser and lounge shirt. . . . *The trouser* in ivory, 138.00. The shirt in nude, 112.00. (Vogue 166/12 (Dec 1, 1976): 9).

(37) Here, she wears wide-cut pants and a belted, rust-colored jacket, both in silk-linen, by Yves Saint Laurent. Jacket (about $1,420) and *trouser* (about $905). (Vogue 185/3 (Mar 1, 1995): 341).

A sense not mentioned in Wickens (1992) is where *trouser* is used to refer to the leg(s) of the garment. Beside examples (7–9) above, we have:

(38) . . . and tried to seize the little dog, but Chrysanthemum grasped him by *the trouser* and tried to drag him down the hall. (Vogue, 17/2 (Jan 10, 1901): xii).

(39) Combination satin corset cover and knickers are also worn, ... One of these in Nattier blue satin, gathered into a band just above the knee, has a down-falling ruffle of white lace, and a second fulled about *the trouser* a bit above the band, (Vogue 30/23 (Dec 5, 1907): 852).

(40) Authentic Highlanders with tapered *trouser*. (Vogue 116/3 (Aug 15, 1950): 74).

(41) Changes in masculine fashions, . . . are certainly less marked than those of feminine attire. An inch or two more or less, added or taken from the coat tails; a longer slope of waist, a greater *width of trouser*, . . ., a higher alti-tude of collar and a more aggressively pointed shoe, are all, . . ., tiny details taken singly, but they stamp the man of fashion and express the vogue of the moment. (Vogue 2/2 (Jul 8, 1893): S12).

Example (41) shows the very first occurrence of *trouser* in the database and is remarkable in several respects. Here the bare NP *trouser* features in a fixed expression "width/length of *trouser*" used in technical jargon for tailored measures. The singular is most likely due to the ellipsis of "leg(s)", which is cognitively the most salient portion of a pair of trousers and is in a way incorporated in the noun modifier *trouser* in the above examples. Through metonymy, the most salient part of the garment has been used to refer to for the whole, as most of our exam-ples show.

The adjectival use of *trouser* is accountable for most occurrences of the singular form in the whole database,[9] but grammar is not the only

---

9   *Trouser* is used attributively 20 times out of 26 in the decade 1892–1902 (e.g., trouser spur, trouser pockets, trouser pattern, trouser crease, trouser seams, trou-ser band, trouser hanger). The plural *trousers* (e.g., *trousers*-pockets, *trousers*-hangers) is also found, but is less frequent.

reason for singular usage in (39–41). This use is also pragmatically and cognitively motivated by the practice of clothing measurements in tailoring, where the body is conceived of as two symmetrical longitudinal halves, as shown by:

(42) … a man at Newport, who wheels in white duck trousers, made very full, like bloomers, and coming <u>to the ankle</u>, (Vogue 6/12 (Sep 19, 1895): 182).

(43) Within the width of 19 ½ inches <u>at knee</u> and 18 ¾ <u>at instep</u>. (Vogue 10/24 (Dec 9, 1897): p. xviii).

(44) The trousers are wide from <u>the hip</u> to <u>the knee</u>, and narrow from the knee to the bottom – (Vogue 8/22 (Dec 3, 1896): 362, vi).

(45) … These cuffs [of chinchilla fur] were fastened upon the outside of <u>the arm</u> almost as high as <u>the shoulder</u>, and they hung to <u>the elbow</u> under <u>the arm</u>. 20/23 (Dec 4, 1902): 862.

Thus, it can be argued that the singular form of bipartite nouns denoting items of clothing (*trouser*) is iconic of how the human body is conceptualized in this specific domain of human activity and discourse. This means that arbitrariness and iconicity are not only culture and language specific but can vary across discourse domains within the same language and culture. The names for body parts occur also in the plural in the database, although their frequency diminishes with the passing of time:

(46) The coat should be made to have square <u>shoulders,</u> … should be cut well in at the waist, and have slightly flaring skirts, falling an inch or two below <u>the knees</u>. (Vogue 15/15 (Apr 12, 1900): iii).

(47) The Tuxedo or dinner coat … comes well over <u>the hips</u>. (Vogue 8/22 (Dec 3, 1896): 362, vi.)

(48) The new geometry [of dress]: swinging wide and hemmed around <u>the knees</u>. (Vogue 206/9 (Sep 1, 2016): 696).

As can be seen from the table below, the Vogue Archive yielded 329 results for "the knees" in the time span 1892–1902 and only 10 results in the time span 2011–2021. The singular "the knee", instead, occurs 503 times between 1892 and 1902 and 49 times between 2011 and 2021. This means that the use of the singular for body parts involved in tailor measurements has always prevailed over the plural in the language of fashion, and has eventually become the default, unmarked grammatical number.[10]

	1892–1902	1950–1960	2011–2021
the knee	503	86	49
the knees	329	70	10
the elbow	713	58	5
the elbows	88	13	1
the ankle	76	62	21
the ankles	62	29	12
the hip	111	77	18
the hips	578	200	10
the calf	46	16	10
the calves	0	3	0
the shoulder	690	129	50
the shoulders	1139	245	27
the foot	396	152	27
the feet	279	39	12
the wrist	425	83	10
the wrists	308	25	4

Table 1: Plural and singular forms of nouns for body parts and number of occurrences in the time spans indicated.

---

10 The marked, exceptional character of plural usage in fashion and clothing is evidenced by the data, where "knees" is used only once (out of 10) as a body reference point for the length of an item of clothing. 9 times out of 10, "the knees" is used to refer to the body parts unrelated to clothing (e.g., the loose skin on the underside of the arms, the crepey skin on the chest, even the wrinkly areas on the knees and elbows. 201/4 (Apr 1, 2011): 224; A pair of Dior heels made her go weak in the knees (201/8 Aug 1, 2011): 96, 98; she moved a bit more slowly, a bit stiffer at the knees. 211/ 11 (Nov 1, 2021): 40).

The same trend of a remarkable majority of singular forms can be observed in Table 1 for nouns denoting other body parts used as reference points in sartorial measurements:[11]

It must be said, though, that the singular form "the knee" has also been dramatically reduced in frequency since the beginning of the 19th century. This can be explained by the progressive transformation of the contents and targets of the magazine, which originally was "a dignified authentic journal of society, fashion and the ceremonial side of life." (Vogue, 1/1 (Dec 17, 1892): 16).

The many illustrations were accompanied by detailed descriptions of clothes, and it was often the case that descriptions made up for the drawings when these were missing. Until photographic reports were introduced, the sections "From our own correspondent" in London and Paris relied on the verbal medium to depict costumes and accessories.[12] As photographs gradually become protagonist and made descriptions redundant and ultimately useless, these are replaced by minimal captions informing about brand and price of clothes. Here are a couple of examples:

(49) Prada coat, polo, turtleneck, bag, gloves, and boots. All clothing and accessories at prada.com. (Vogue 211/9 (Sep 1, 2021): 300).

(50) True colors: from left: 3.1 Phillip Lim coat ($2,500) and pants ($450); 3.1 Phillip Lim, nyc. Dkny blazer, $345; select Dkny stores. Yigal Azrouël pants ($495). Orange coat ($1,695), and white pants ($595); yigalazrouel. com. (Vogue 201/9 (Sep 1, 2011): 578, 582).

---

11   The trend is stable over time except for two items (i.e., hip(s) and shoulder(s)) displaying what we may term a "markedness reversal", until at least the 1960s.

12   From December 1897 to December 1910 there is even a section entitled "Description(s) of Fashions" / "Fashion Descriptions", while the sections "Whispers" and "Smart fashion(s) for limited incomes"/"Dressing on a limited income" (Jan 1898 - Nov 1922) give suggestions on how to realise inexpensive but effective clothes. In this connection, it can be noted that from March 1899 to December 1919 Vogue published one pattern a week (the first pattern was a model of a "drop skirt") which could be purchased from Vogue by sending coupons. This section was clearly meant for seamstresses, milliners and dressmakers, who formed part of Vogue's readership.

5. Conclusions

This chapter has explored the grammatical and semantic aspects of bipartite garment nouns used as singulars in the language of fashion by focusing on the lexical item *trouser(s)*. Data extracted from *The Vogue Archive* (America) has allowed me to challenge the claim that bipartites are *pluralia tantum* nouns, that is, nouns that can only occur in the plural. In fact, *trousers* has passed the same tests for countability that *scissors* failed (Allan 1980), which encourages a reassessment of its grammatical status as "plural dominant" rather than "plural only".

Data also allowed me to challenge the categorical statement whereby bipartites can only express generic reference to type, model, or style when they are used as singulars (Wickens (1992); Payne & Huddleston (2002)). A few cases were found of *trouser* mostly used in captions with specific, indexical reference to the item portrayed in the picture.

A type of reference emerged from the data which, to the best of my knowledge, is not mentioned in the literature, i.e., reference to one leg of a pair of trousers. This type of reference, it is argued, is cognitively grounded in the way of conceptualizing the human body in this specific domain of human activity and is reflected in language. This seems to question the notion of the arbitrariness of the singular (*trouser*) implicit in the claim about the iconicity of the plural for bipartites (Wierzbicka 1988), and suggests that iconicity can also have a local, discourse-specific validity.

References

Allan, Keith. 1980. Nouns and countability. *Language* 56(3): 541–567.

Baayen, Harald R., Ton Dijkstra, and Robert Schreuder. 1997. Singulars and plurals in Dutch: Evidence for a parallel dual route model. *Journal of Memory and Language* 37: 94–117.

Carter, Ronald and Michael McCarthy. 2006. *Cambridge Grammar of English*. Cambridge: Cambridge University Press.

Chierchia, Gennaro. 1998. "Plurality of mass nouns and the notion of 'semantic parameter' ". In Susan Rothstein (ed.), *Events and Grammar*. Dordrecht: Kluwer, 53–103.

Corbett, Greville. 2019. Pluralia tantum nouns and the theory of features: A typology of nouns with noncanonical number properties. *Morphology* 29(1): 51–108.

Gleason, Henry Allan. 1961. *An Introduction to Descriptive Linguistics*. Revised edition. New York: Holt, Rinehart and Winston.

Langacker, Ronald Wayne. 1987. *Foundations of Cognitive Grammar: Theoretical Prerequisites,* vol. I. Stanford: Stanford University Press.

Mencken, Henry Louis. 1963. *The American Language: An Inquiry into the Development of English in the United States.* The fourth edition and the two supplements, abridged, with annotations and new material, by Raven I. McDavid, Jr., with the assistance of David W. Maurer. New York: Alfred A. Knopf.

Nenonen, Marja and Jussi Niemi. 2010. Mismatches between grammatical number and conceptual numerosity: A number-decision experiment on collective nouns, number neutralization, pluralia tantum, and idiomatic plurals. *Folia Linguistica* 44: 103–125.

Nickels, Lindsey, Britta Biedermánn, Nora Fieder, and Niels O. Schiller. 2015. The lexical-syntactic representation of number. *Language, Cognition and Neuroscience* 30(3): 287–304.

Payne, John and Rodney Huddleston. 2002. "Nouns and noun phrases". In Huddleston, Rodney and Geoffrey K. Pullum (eds.), *The Cambridge Grammar of the English Language*. Cambridge: Cambridge University Press.

Quirk, Randolph, Sidney Greenbaum, Geoffrey Leech, and Jan Svartvik. 1985. *A Comprehensive Grammar of the English Language*. London: Longman.

Wickens, Mark. 1992. *Grammatical Number in English Nouns: An Empirical and Theoretical Account*. Amsterdam: Benjamins.

Wierzbicka, Anna. 1988. *The Semantics of Grammar*. Amsterdam: Benjamins.

Wierzbicka, Anna. 1991. Semantic rules know no exceptions. *Studies in Language* 15: 371–398.

Williams, Edwin. 1994. Remarks on lexical knowledge. *Lingua* 92, 7–
     34.

Wisniewski, Edward J. 2010. On using count nouns, mass nouns, and
     pluralia tantum: What counts? In Francis Jeffry Pelletier (ed.),
     Kinds, Things, and Stuff: Mass Terms and Generics. Oxford: Oxford
     University Press, 166–190.

ANNALISA BAICCHI

Clothes We Dress In. The Conceptualisation of Fashion Terms

1. Introduction

The clothes we dress in unveil our social status, pre-empt our ideological position, and pass on our self-presentation, beliefs, and values.

Fashion is a form of communication loaded with cultural meanings and social values, as Barthes theorised in 1967 when he applied de Saussure's structural semiotics to his discussion of the fashion system. His contribution was fundamental for making a parallel between two semiotic systems. Just as Saussure distinguished language into *langue* (system) and *parole* (use), Barthes distinguished fashion into *dress* (the system) and *dressing* (the real clothes). The dress system encompasses the semiotic meaning that clothes prompt as well as the guidelines that govern their matching, while dressing refers to the real apparel we wear.

The clothes we dress in can be defined as a theatrical representation of our beliefs, social status, and power. In keeping with Conceptual Metaphor Theory (Lakoff and Johnson 1980), Kövecses introduces the foundational metaphor LIFE IS A SHOW OR SPECTACLE (2005: 184). By endorsing his proposal and paraphrasing the Shakespearean line that "All world's a stage" (*As You Like It* II, VII, 139), we can devise the CLOTHES ARE STAGE COSTUMES metaphor, a stage where we wear costumes that enable us to perform and make manifest our role, thus communicating our personal message.

This chapter investigates English clothing terms and proposes a qualitative analysis through the lens of Cognitive Linguistics while considering the cultural references that those terms may suggest.

The dataset of clothing terms has been assembled manually gathering lexemes from *The Fairchild Dictionary of Fashion* (henceforth, DoF; Tortora & Keiser 2014), with a view to showing how such terms are coined in accordance with concepts related to spatial, situational, and cultural experiences.

We state beforehand that meaning is not contained in the linguistic items, but it is constructed in the speakers' mind (Radden et al. 2007: 1). Lexemes prompt meaningful conceptual representations, but, along with linguistic knowledge, we also need encyclopaedic knowledge to achieve meaning representations, as theoretical frameworks like Frame Semantics (Fillmore 1982), Idealised Cognitive Models (Lakoff 1987), and Mental Spaces (Fauconnier 1994) have distinctly demonstrated. As lexical items are points of access to encyclopaedic knowledge, a principled distinction between semantics and pragmatics is unsustainable.

With this premise being established, the qualitative analysis of fashion lexemes is couched in the belief that language is the manifestation of both natural and cultural phenomena, the arena where patterns of biological experience, social interaction, and cognitive processes intertwine in dynamic and complex ways (Baicchi 2015). The language of fashion is no exception, as it mirrors both the cultural habits of wearers and their conceptual system (Lakoff 1987; Sharifian 2008, 2011). Moving from the tenet that communication merges the three semiotic systems of language, cognition, and culture, this study endorses the theoretical principles of Cognitive Semantics, according to which cognitive reality is the outcome of culture, and language is intimately structured and bound to embodied experience (Johnson 2007). More specifically, the English clothing terminology is explored with the aim of identifying the conceptual operations that motivate the coinage of fashion lexemes and their cultural load.

The chapter is organised as follows. Section 2 focuses on the notions of categorisation and prototypicality in thought and language. Section 3 explores how the coinage of clothing terms is the outcome of the interplay between cognition and culture, and describes the tripartite taxonomy of such terms as has been recently proposed by the 'Word Design Theory'; it then examines the cognitive and cultural grounding of clothing terms, and identifies in the four 'Idealised Cognitive Models' the mental processes that enable meaning extensions of fashion lexemes; finally, it shows how cultural conceptualisations are necessary to grasp the meaning of more complex terms. Section 4 discusses the dataset taking into count the different cognitive and cultural grounding.

Section 5 merges all the lines together with the aim of pinning down the different degrees of cognitive and cultural complexity of clothing terms. Section 6 offers some conclusive remarks and hints at future implications.

2. Categorisation in thought and language

Concepts in our mind and their expression in language are closely interwoven and mediated by means of cognitive processes, such as the formation of categories, their grouping, and their extension through metonymic and metaphoric operations. The categories that our mind identifies within an ecological system involve "imaginative structures of understanding, such as schemata, metaphor, metonymy, and mental imagery" (Johnson 1987: xi).

Importantly, as Harnad (2005: 21) clearly states, "categorization is any systematic differential interaction between an autonomous, adaptive sensorimotor system and its world". This entails that categorisation is biased by the perceiver's personal interpretation of reality, and it equates to "the interpretation of experience with respect to previously existing structures" (Langacker 2008: 17). The ability to categorise corresponds to determine whether a specific item is an instance of one category or another. To put it with Croft and Cruse, "categorization involves the apprehension of some individual entity, some particular of experience, as an instance of something conceived more abstractly that also encompasses other actual and potential instantiations" (2004: 74). Very simply defined, categorisation is the cognitive ability to draw conceptual boundaries and give structure to the world we live in. This does not mean that our conceptual distinctions can be fully represented by linguistic categories, since language can verbalise only a small part of our conceptual distinctions (Radden and Dirven 2007). When conceptual categories are expressed as linguistic categories, they are grouped into lexical categories, and when they denote specific conceptual content, they are grouped into grammatical categories that provide the structural scaffold of language.

Lexical categories are specifically investigated in this chapter through exemplifications drawn from the language of fashion, and to do so, we also need to touch upon the notion of 'prototypicality'. The way in which we experience reality and mentally represent it occur by making use of a 'prototype', that is, an abstract mental representation that gathers the core features that best represent instances of a given category. The prototype categorisation model, or Prototype Theory developed by Rosch and colleagues (Rosch 1977; Rosch and Mervis 1975; Mervis and Rosch 1981), distinguishes human categories into two types of members: the 'prototype', that is, the core exemplar that better exemplifies the category, and several peripheral members related to the core member in a motivated way. Hence, the members of lexical categories may have a different status: Some are core members, which are more representative and salient (e.g. *pants*), while others are peripheral members, that is, less representative and less frequently used (e.g. *Capri pants*). A specific type of garment, let's say *pleated skirt*, can be understood as an instantiation of the category SKIRT, which in turn is the conceptual category of this abstract mental construct.

Although categorisation is often automatic and unconscious, there are questionable cases. Since language can offer only a small fraction of our conceptual distinctions, sometimes it is vague in its description of reality (Geeraerts et al. 1994). If we consider the clothing term *culottes*, we may hesitate in attributing it to one category or another. We should ask ourselves whether they are a type of pants or skirt: In this case, *culottes* are a subordinate term of skirt and pants respectively. We may even judge it necessary to create a separate category of garment that covers legs, and, in this case, *culottes* would be a basic level term defining a category at the same level as skirt and pants, with the three of them belonging the same conceptual domain of covering-leg garment.

3. Cognition and culture in fashion language

The coinage of clothing lexemes largely results from the semantic interplay between culture and cognition (Biscetti and Baicchi 2019).

The cultural connotation of fashion terms may be exemplified by the culturally loaded compound *Capri pants*: a full understanding of this compound involves the cultural knowledge of the place of origin of this garment and the person, the actress Brigitte Bardot, who made this type of pants famous in the 1950s.

Spatial cognition is instead involved any time the understanding of a fashion lexeme relies on the conceptualisation of the body and its arrangement in space. Terms such as *underskirt* and *off-the-shoulder dress* are compounds where the locative prepositions point to the spatial relation that the cloth holds with the part of the body where it must be worn. As such terms are coined in accordance with concepts related to cultural and spatial experience, fashion language appears to conflate the perception of our body both in the spatial and in the cultural extent.

Having set that language combines the two realms of culture and cognition, it is not unreasonable to analyse clothing terminology making use of some theoretical notions belonging to Cognitive Linguistics and Cultural Linguistics. Indeed, the terms used to talk about clothes mirror both the conceptual system of its speakers/wearers (Johnson 2007) and the culture in which cognition is rooted (Sharifian 2011).

In the ensuing sub-sections, the 'Word Design Theory' (Catricalà 2017) is first introduced (2.1), which offers a useful taxonomy of fashion lexemes; such a classification is then broadened by making use of basic notions in Cognitive Linguistics (2.2), namely the "Idealised Cognitive Models" (Lakoff 1987), and in Cultural Linguistics (2.3), specifically the notion of "Cultural Conceptualisations" (Sharifian 2017).

3.1 The word design theory

In her research on fashion language, Catricalà (2017) has recently proposed a tripartite classification of clothing terms, which she labels 'Word Design Theory', based on the type of function and informative load that those terms contain. Three main classes of lexemes are identified: instruction words, description words, and narration words.

To the first type belong compounds such as *underskirt* and *overblouse*, which contain the instruction where to put on those garments, that is, *under* or *over* some other cloth.

The class of description words indicates the use for which the garment has been designed. For example, the term *boat-shoes* points to the specific situation where that footwear should be put on: in this case, the core meaning of the term describes the function of *boat-shoes* with respect to other types of footwear, such as *running shoes, slingback shoes,* or *platform shoes,* which play different functions.

Finally, the class of narration words tell us something about the history, production, or culture that are connected to the apparel. The term *Chanel suit,* the classic women's collarless jacket designed by Gabrielle Chanel in the 1920s, involves the knowledge of its origin, its stylist, and its cultural connotations, such as elegance and glamour.

Table 1 exemplifies fashion lexemes subdivided into the three staple classes.

Instruction word	*overcoat; underskirt; across-the-shoulder bag; off-the-shoulder dress; overboots.*
Descriptive word	*courier bag; doctor bag; cabin-boy breeches; attaché case; cathedral train; bell sleeve; fishtail skirt.*
Narrative word	*Capri pants; cardigan; Eaton jacket; Macintosh; Peter Pan collar; Wellington boots.*

Table 1. *Tripartite classification of clothing terms*

Overall, the three main aspects of instructing, describing, and narrating clearly exemplify how we may classify clothing terms: respectively, they highlight the part of the body the garment is for, the relationship with similar clothes or accessories, and the origin or tradition specifying a given socio-cultural context.

After sketching the tripartite subdivision of fashion lexemes, we turn to discuss how clothing terms are grounded in cognition and culture.

3.2 *Cognitive grounding of clothing lexemes*

We said that one crucial cognitive process in the coinage of any type of lexemes is 'categorisation'. When innovations occur in the reality, new conceptual categories are created along with new lexical categories.

Instead of coining brand new terms to name new entities, the meaning of existing linguistic categories is extended through conceptual shifting, mainly metonymy and metaphor, that we use to elaborate existing knowledge structures (Lipka 1992). In other words, our mind relies on the process of categorisation to draw conceptual boundaries between experiences and objects, and to conceptualise a set of similar entities that are relevant and meaningful in a speech community. Any category is a part of an overall system of categories. For example, the three terms *miniskirt, pleated skirt,* and *wrap-over skirt* are exemplars of 'skirt' at the basic level of significance and of 'women's garment' at the higher level of the garment hierarchy (Geeraerts et al. 1994).

The coinage of lexemes and their meaning extension are mainly motivated by metonymic and metaphoric operations, that is, by projecting, or mapping one set of conceptual entities onto another set of entities. To mention a pair of examples, metonymy maps one entity onto another within the same domain, as in *board shorts,* a type of shorts for swimming or surfing; while metaphor maps the structure of one domain onto another domain, as in *north-south bag,* where the cardinal points of the earth domain are used to name a bag that is vertical in shape, longer than it is large.

However, to grasp how human beings categorise entities, organise their conceptual representation, and give names to them, reference to the whole set of the "Idealised Cognitive Models" (hereafter, ICMs) is necessary. As Lakoff (1987) explains, ICMs are four principled-governed cognitive structures –frames, embodied schemas, metonymy, and metaphor– that are idealised to understand the world and to represent it conceptually by merging aspects of our experience and enhancing conceptual inferences. Patently, ICMs are not real, but they are a model that tries to schematise reality; they are cognitive as they are construed in the mind; and they are idealised for they abstract regularities from experience. Broadly defined, ICMs are gestalts, or complex structured wholes employed by our mind to organise knowledge. A distinction is here necessary: while frames and embodied schemas consist of stored information and are therefore non-operational ICMs, metonymy and metaphor are operational ICMs because they exploit the non-operational ones to engender productive cognitive operations (Baicchi & Ruiz de Mendoza 2010; Ruiz de Mendoza & Baicchi 2007).

To detail a bit, frames are cognitive representations of the real world and are a part of the encyclopaedic knowledge. They are a structured set of interconnected concepts that are formed through inductive generalisation of extralinguistic knowledge. By way of exemplification, the compound *Eton jacket* entails the activation of a multi-faceted frame capable of combining the lexical meaning of *jacket* with the cultural knowledge of the famous British college where students wear it. Likewise, the compound *Lennon specs*, originally English workmen's sunglasses with circular metal rimmed lenses and metal temples, requires the knowledge of the singer John Lennon who made them popular in the 1960s.

Embodied schemas, the other type of non-operational schemas, emerge from bodily experience and prompt the formation of general categories and complex concepts. They are abstract, pre-conceptual, and topological patterns of experience, such as spatial orientation (*front-back, up-down, left-right, inside-outside*) and the path schema (e.g., *from, across, to*). Clothing terms motivated by embodied schemas are immediately meaningful to us. Such terms make ample use of locative and directional prepositions, as in *topcoat* or *undershirt*, which point to the part of the body where the garment is worn.

Metonymy is an operational ICM that enhances the conceptualisation of one entity highlighting its relation to something else. Being an intra-domain mapping based on the general principle of contiguity, the term *beach dress* makes explicit the place where it is worn, and it also indicates the relationship between this type of dress with other types in the beachwear domain. This term is motivated by the PLACE FOR FUNCTION metonymy: the place *beach* is mentioned to point to the function of the garment, that is, to cover part of the body while sunbathing. Another example is the term *thigh boots*, which is motivated by the PART OF THE BODY FOR MEASURE metonymy, where the thigh is mentioned to indicate the measure of the boots.

Metaphor, the other operational ICM, is an inter-domain mapping, based on the general principle of similarity, that enacts a set of correspondences across two conceptual domains. For example, the term *east-west bag* projects the cardinal points of the earth domain onto those of a bag that is horizontal in shape, larger than it is long. Another interesting term is *butterfly sleeve*: at the metaphorical level, it maps the shape of a butterfly's wings onto the shape of the dress' sleeves, and it is motivated by the SLEEVES ARE WINGS metaphor.

Table 2 diagrams the four ICMs while exemplifying each type with some clothing terms from the dataset.

ICMs			
"non-operational ICMs"		**"operational ICMs"**	
Frame	**Embodied schema**	**Metonymy**	**Metaphor**
Capri pants; cardigan; Sam Browne belt; Oxonian shoe; Eaton jacket; Macintosh; Eugénie hat; Chanel suit; Chesterfield coat; Kelly bag; Peter Pan collar;	*overcoat; underskirt; overboots; across-the-shoulder bag; off-the-shoulder dress; wrap-over skirt; leggings; overblouse; undershirt; cross-body bag; backpack.*	*boat-shoes; spacesuit; car coat; beach dress; knapsack; courier bag; doctor bag; cabin-boy breeches; attaché case; cathedral train; camouflage suit; knee pants; ankle socks; elbow gloves.*	*east-west bag; north-south bag; bell sleeve; fishtail skirt; batwing sleeve; butterfly sleeve;*

Table 2. *ICMs motivating clothing terms*

3.3 Cultural grounding of clothing lexemes

The coinage of clothing terms and the full grasp of their meaning involve not only cognition but also culture. Cultural Linguistics is therefore a relevant theoretical framework that, along with Cognitive Linguistics, offers suitable tools for our analysis. Cultural Linguistics, as was defined by its founding father, Farzad Sharifian, explores

> "the conceptualizations that have a cultural basis and are encoded in and com-municated through features of human languages. The pivotal focus on meaning as conceptualisation in Cultural Linguistics owes its centrality to cognitive lin-guistics, a discipline that Cultural Linguistics drew on at its inception." (Shari-fian 2015: 473).

Sharifian revised the notion of culture in favour of a culturally grounded conceptualisation of experience and introduced the notion of 'cultural cognition'. This notion combines cultural conceptualisations and language: namely, language is entrenched in cultural conceptualisations and, at the same time, units of cultural conceptualisations, which are linked to some features of the linguistic organisation, include the three classes of cultural schemas, cultural categories, and cultural metaphors. We will see that these three classes can be usefully applied to the analysis of clothing terms, even though not exhaustively. We will in fact add one more type to Sharifian's taxonomy, that is, cultural metonymies, which motivate some types of fashion compounds.

Cultural schemas enable us to analyse "features of human languages in relation to the cultural conceptualisations in which they are entrenched" (Sharifian 2017: 39). The label 'schema' refers to those mental structures that are necessary to organise knowledge and consists of elements working together to process information. We store cultural schemas in our memory and rely on them to figure out new knowledge from past experiences. For example, a term like *Birkin bag* requires us to have access to the cultural knowledge of the British-born and Paris-based actress Jane Birkin, who, on board an Air France plane, designed that bag together with Jean-Louise Dumas, the Chief Executive of Hermès; but we may also need to know the cultural schema that distinguishes the *Birkin bag* from the very similar *Kelly bag*, after the name of actress Princess Grace Kelly, with the latter bag fitting a more elegant style than the former.

Cultural categories, as the name suggests, refer to the use of those categories that are shared in a cultural group and associated with language. Many components of experience like objects, events, settings, mental states, properties, and relations are cultural categories that human beings acquire and interiorise with very little instruction through normal exposure over their life (Glushko et al. 2008: 129; Sharifian 2017: 43), as is the case with embodied schemas. For example, *elbow gloves* and *ankle socks* are understood with little effort based on the knowledge of the parts of our body and the space that they occupy. In these examples, *elbow* and *ankle* profile the measure of the two garments: a pair of gloves that reach the elbow, and a pair of short socks that cover the ankles only.

Cultural metaphors, i.e., "conceptual metaphors that are culturally constructed" (Sharifian 2017: 45), motivate such lexemes like *fishtail skirt* and *batwing sleeves*. To grasp the meaning of these compounds, an inter-domain mapping process is necessary. The skirt is mapped onto a fish, suggesting that the shape of the skirt resembles the tail of a fish. Through a similar analogic process, *batwing sleeves* are sleeves with a deep armhole and a tight wrist that are mapped onto the shape of the animal's wings.

Cultural metonymies, which we add to the list proposed by Sharifian, motivate compounds such as *Wellington boots* and *Peter Pan collar*. These garments are metonymic exemplars of the categories of boots and collars; at the same time, the modifying constituents point to cultural frames referring, respectively, to the 1st Duke of Wellington, who popularised this type of military riding boot, and to the actress Maude Adams, who designed and worn that collar in 1905 when she starred Barries' play "Peter Pan".

Table 3 exemplifies clothing terminology while grouping some terms into the three types of cultural conceptualisations proposed by Sharifian. As for cultural categories, we have subdivided them into embodied and metonymic categories, whereby the former encompasses terms that need recourse to the notion of embodiment to be fully understood, while the latter specifies fashion lexemes that are metonymic instances of the more general category of garments.

cultural schemas	*Capri pants; cardigan; Oxonian shoe; Sam Browne belt; Kelly bag; Eaton jacket; Macintosh; Eugénie hat; Peter Pan collar; Chesterfield coat.*
cultural categories	*overcoat; underskirt; overboots; across-the-shoulder bag; off-the-shoulder dress; wrap-over skirt; leggings; undershirt; cross-body bag; overblouse; backpack.*
cultural metonymy	*boat-shoes; car coat; spacesuit; beach dress; Eaton jacket; Wellington boots; courier bag; doctor bag; cabin-boy breeches; attaché case; knee pants; ankle socks; elbow gloves; cathedral train; camouflage suit; rain hat.*
cultural metaphor	*north-south bag; east-west bag; bell sleeve; batwing sleeve; butterfly sleeve; fishtail skirt.*

Table 3. Cultural conceptualisations of clothing terms

The different types of cultural conceptualisations are not always separate classes, but they may intertwine in many ways. For instance, while the clothing term *spacesuit* simply evokes a cultural metonymic category, as it points to a type of suit that can be worn in a specific situation, a term like *Sam Browne belt* involves both a metonymic category and a cultural schema: it is in fact related to metonymy since it is a type of leather belt, one running diagonally across the chest from the left side of the body over the right shoulder; and, at the same time, it points to the British Indian Army General Sir Samuel James Browne, who created it in the 19th century. Another example may be the word *butterfly sleeve*: it is a metonymic exemplar of sleeve, and its name is coined metaphorically through the mapping of the shape of the sleeve onto the wings of a butterfly; in addition, the term also points to the cultural schema of a particular national costume worn by women of the Philippines. Finally, the *elbow gloves* compound is metonymic for it specifies a type of gloves, it is motivated by the notion of embodiment whereby *elbow* hints at the length of the gloves, which go from the fingers and hands and cover the elbow, and its full understanding involves the cultural schema referring to its use in a formal situation.

4. Cognitive and cultural analyses of data

This section discusses further examples from the dataset, and, only for the purpose of analysis, compounds are grouped based on the prevalent ICM that motivate them.

Clothing terms licensed by the non-operational ICMs (frames and embodied schemas) are considered before those instantiated by the operational ones (metonymy and metaphor). Surely, this does not mean that the cognitive and cultural grounding of each group does not interweave with the others; it simply means that one type of motivation is more (or less) relevant for the grasping of the semantic outcome of fashion lexemes.

4.1 Frame-based compounds

Clothing terms in this group can be fully understood with systematic recourse to the encyclopaedic knowledge. In most cases, they are structurally formed by the noun designating the apparel which is premodified by a noun referring to a place (*Capri pants*), or a person (*Kelly bag*), but they may be simplexes coinciding with a proper name (*cardigan, macintosh*).

Consider headwear compounds. They provide examples with different degrees of cultural knowledge necessary to identify specific items. For example, *Garbo hat* explicitly refers to a specific and easily understandable apparel, a hat, which is to be combined with the cultural schema related to the actress Greta Garbo, the famous Swedish-born film star who would put on a slouch hat in the 1930s.

A similar process is at work when the lexeme *hat* is combined with a proper name, like *Rex Harrison hat*, a man's hat made of wool tweed with narrow snap-brim, which was popularised in 1956 when the actor Rex Harrison worn it in his role of Professor Henry Higgings in the musical *My Fair Lady*. Instead, *Merry Widow hat*, a very wide-brimmed velvet hat ornated with ostrich plumes, points to the title of the light opera set to music by Franz Lehár in 1905.

More complex is the meaning of *Fedora*. It is a hat, but this piece of information is not contained in the simplex, and therefore deep encyclopaedic knowledge is necessary to understand what the label refers to. *Fedora* is a man's felt hat, nowadays worn also by women, which has a brim and high crown with a crease from front to back; it was named after the female protagonist of Sardou's play titled 'Fedora'.

4.2 Embodied schemas-based compounds

Embodied schemas are cognitive mappings that involve the spatial relations between the garment and the body, as in *underskirt* or *off-the-shoulder-dress*. Compounds motivated by embodied schemas have a Preposition + Noun structure (P+N), which is quite frequent in the lexicon of fashion, and their meaning and function can be easily identified. The P+N construction (in the sense of Goldberg 1995; see also Booij 2010) is an exocentric compound, where the preposition is a locative particle, expressing a spatial relation: it in fact conveys a pure locative meaning as the one that particles express when used as free morphemes (adverb or preposition).

Consider the term *underskirt*. It is "a simple basic skirt over which an overskirt, or drapery, hangs" (DoF). This is the case in which the compound explicitly indicates the spatial orientation related to the garment.

The instruction word *turn-over collar* indicates that the collar of a pullover must be rolled and turned over the neck; while the label *across-the-shoulder bag* gives the instruction that the handbag must be looped over the shoulder and across the trunk by a strap.

Other lexemes can be quite simple to understand, as *back-of-the-head hat*, which gives very precise instruction how the hat must be worn, i.e., in a way that it covers the back of the head. The spatial preposition in the lexeme *overshoes* describes a "waterproof fabric or rubber shoe worn over other shoes in inclement weather" (DoF).

However, there are clothing terms where the locative particle may be misleading, as in the case of *overcoat*. This might be wrongly interpreted as a coat that must be worn over another coat. It is instead a "man's coat, heavier than a topcoat, designed for very cold weather. Sometimes lined with fur or modacrylic pile and made in any of a variety of styles." (DoF). In this case *over* plays almost the function of a prefix, used here to convey a scalar meaning, and to suggest that this type of coat is a cloth that can protect better than other types from severe winter temperatures (Biscetti and Baicchi 2019).

4.3 Metonymy-based compounds

Metonymy-based compounds prompt an interpretation that involves intra-domain mappings based on the association between two concepts. This type of compounds is realised as a Noun + Noun construction, where the first constituent prompts the activation of an ICM that allows for mental access to the compound head. Consider *spacesuit*: it indicates a garment to be worn in a very specific circumstance; in addition, it is metonymic for it is included into the category of suits at the basic level of significance and occupies the lower level of specificities in the garment hierarchy.

Another example is *car coat*, a "sport or utility coat made hip- to three-quarter length, which is comfortable for driving a car" (DoF). The modifier *car* prompts the cognitive operation of 'domain reduction', which gives "conceptual prominence to part of a concept" (Ruiz de Mendoza and Galera 2014: 92), that is, it reduces the ample concept of coat to a specific type.

Metonymy reduction is at work also in compounds such as *doctor bag, cabin-boy breeches*, and *camouflage suit* that specify the function they entail, and they are motivated by the PROFESSION FOR STYLE metonymy.

Similar lexemes, such as *stadium coat, duffel coat*, and *ranch coat* are licensed by the PLACE FOR STYLE metonymy, which specifies the circumstance when the garments are worn.

Compounds such as *knee pants* and *wrist gloves* are motivated by the PART OF THE BODY FOR MEASURE metonymy. In fact, *knee pants* are "pants of varying widths fastened below knee" (DoF), while *wrist gloves* are "short gloves ending with a wrist bone" (DoF).

Finally, consider *Wellington boots*. This compound exemplifies the case in which both domain reduction and cultural frame are combined. First, we understand that the boots the compound refers to are a specific type of boots, that is, there is a process of domain reduction in the boot category; then, the modifier Wellington is correctly interpreted if we know that specific type of boots, the calf-length boot, was named after the Duke of Wellington, who defeated Napoleon in the battle of Waterloo. Overall, the fashion lexeme is instantiated by the PERSON FOR STYLE metonymy.

4.4 Metaphor-based compounds

Conceptual metaphor instantiates an analogy relation between two concepts. The two constituents of the N+N compound hold a similarity association between the garment domain and another domain specified by the modifier constituent.

Consider clothing terms like *elephant sleeve* and *kangaroo skirt*. An *elephant sleeve* is a large sleeve hanging down from the shoulder in the shape of an elephant's ear: thus, the sleeve is mapped onto the animal's ear. Likewise, the name *trumpet skirt*, a straight skirt flaring at the hem resembling an inverted trumpet, is motivated by the metaphoric projection from the skirt domain onto that of the musical instrument.

The nominal compound *bell sleeve* describes a type of sleeve that has a shape reminiscent of a bell. This clothing term has been coined in analogy with a chiming bell, which has involved the activation of a metaphoric mapping.

An image metaphor is needed to grasp the meaning of *petal collar*. This is a "collar several irregularly shaped pieces that look like petals of a flower" (DoF). The compound is motivated by the COLLAR IS A PETAL metaphor.

5. Degrees of conceptual complexity

We have seen that both non-operational and operational ICMs are cognitive tools that are entrenched in our mind, but they display different degrees of conceptual complexity. We now discuss how clothing terms can be accommodated along a cline of conceptual complexity, and how they intertwine with cultural conceptualisations.

Embodied schemas emerge at a very early age in our infancy when new-borns form pre-conceptual gestalt structures of animate and inanimate entities through the senses. Given their strong entrenchment in our brain and mind, embodied schemas are said to be universally shared across human beings, even when they belong to distant cultures. As Johnson (1987: 62) explains,

> "because our bodies are very much alike with respect to their physiological makeup, we would expect to find commonly shared (if not universal) gestalt structures for many of our physical interactions within our environment".

As embodied schemas are universal and entrenched in our mind, they are the least complex type of ICM (*undershirt*) and the least cultural. At higher levels of complexity are metonymy and metaphor. Metonymy, being a matter of contiguity (*raincoat*), is easier to identify than metaphor, which instead requires the ability to pin down similarity between the elements of two different domains (*bat sleeves*). The most complex ICM is the frame, for its understanding requires to pin down cultural information through shared knowledge and personal experience without which the meaning of the compound is partially opaque (*Kelly bag*), or totally opaque (*Macintosh*).

With reference to Catricalà's tripartite taxonomy of fashion words, clothing terms belonging to the instruction class, that is, P+V compounds (*overblouse*) and V+N compounds (*turn-over collar, wrap-over skirt*) score the lowest degree of semantic complexity, because the locative particles explicitly refer to the spatial extent. Instead, N+N instruction words (*spacesuit, car coat, knee pants*) are motivated by conceptual metonymy and are therefore more complex lexemes to understand, as they can be fully interpreted through recourse to cultural categories. In addition, in the light of Prototype Theory discussed in section 2, suit is a more representative and salient member of the lexical category, while *spacesuit, Eton suit, camouflage suit,* and *sailor suit* are more specific, hence more peripheral, and less representative.

At a higher level of complexity are descriptive words. For instance, the nominal compound *cathedral train* describes an "elongated back portion of woman's skirt that lies on the floor and is pulled along behind by wearer" (DoF). This clothing term illustrates the interplay of the two operational ICMs. On the one side, the compound is motivated by the PLACE FOR LENGTH metonymy, based on the conceptual contiguity between the cathedral and the length of its nave, onto which the length of the bride's train is mapped. On the other side, the modifier constituent *cathedral* is the reference point that triggers the wedding ceremony frame and the script according to which weddings celebrated in a cathedral require apparel of great importance, and for the bride a very long, therefore, important train, along the lines of the IMPORTANT IS BIG metaphor (Ruiz de Mendoza and Galera 2014). Image metaphors license descriptive words, as in the case of *trumpet skirt*, which is motivated by projection of the skirt domain onto that of the musical instrument.

Narrative words are coined with an eye to the story of the origin of garments and can be understood only with recourse to the cultural frame they evoke. To understand the meaning of terms like *Chesterfield coat* and *Oxonian shoes* we need to know something about their cultural history. *Chesterfield coat* is a straight-cut overcoat with black velvet collar named after the 6th Earl of Chesterfield, while *Oxonian shoes* are a type of shoes worn by students at the University of Oxford. These narrative words are coined by extending the meanings of existing lexical categories (*coat, shoe*). Similarly, the garment called *cardigan* is named after the 7th Earl of Cardigan, who wore such a jacket in the Crimean War. A full understanding of narrative words is prompted by cultural schemas, which we store in our mind and enable us to acquire new knowledge from past experiences.

6. Conclusion

The clothes we dress in disclose our culture, beliefs and social status, and the names that we use to talk about them hint at the cognitive operations that motivate their coinage. This chapter has attempted to illustrate the meaning construction of some English fashion lexemes retrieved from one of the most accredited dictionaries, *The Fairchild Dictionary of Fashion*, and to identify the degree of conceptual complexity that those terms entail.

As is usual for dictionaries, entries are arranged in alphabetical order or grouped into categories, such as headwear, footwear, or scarves. This chapter has suggested an alternative way of grouping lexemes into cognitively motivated categories, with the belief that this may enhance the full understanding of their meaning. This is the main idea that has backboned our proposal.

In the chapter sections, we have first described the tripartite taxonomy recently proposed by Catricalà (2017), who groups fashion words into instruction, description, and narration, depending on the different function that clothing terms contain, more or less explicitly. We have then made a step forward and analysed a sample of fashion lexemes based on the cognitive operations that motivate each term. We have pursued this goal relying on some of the core tenets in Cognitive Linguistics (categorisation, idealised cognitive models) and analysed compounds in the four categories of frames, embodied schemas, metonymy, and metaphor. We have also taken into count Cultural Linguistics (cultural conceptualisations) and its taxonomy of cultural schemas and categories. These analyses have prompted the discussion of clothing terminology in terms of conceptual complexity.

We hope we have shown with sufficient clarity that terms motivated by embodied schemas, which are universal and well entrenched in our mind, accommodates at the lowest level of conceptual complexity when they denote compounds formed by locative particles (*overskirt*); they also occupy the lowest grade along the scale of cultural complexity. When fashion lexemes are motivated by metonymy, they are conceptually more complex; metaphorically motivated terms are even more complex and accommodate at a higher level than the metonymic ones. Finally, lexemes motivated by cultural frames are the most complex in general, and more specifically, compounds (*Kelly bag*) are less complex than simplexes (*cardigan*).

The conceptual operations we have dealt with instantiate the construction of meaningful lexemes used to denote the clothes we dress in. We think that the study we have conducted and described in these few pages, besides the identification of how our mind categorise experience and verbalise it, may be of some help in the design and production of glossaries and dictionaries that go beyond the traditional list of entries in alphabetical order. It may be helpful —for instance, for lexicographers and fashion studies students— to classify terms in the light of their conceptual and cultural complexity, which have the advantage of enhancing easier categorisation processes and faster memorisation. This future implication that we wish for will no doubt require further investigation based on a larger dataset retrieved from a range of specialised dictionaries and corpora.

References

Baicchi, Annalisa. 2015. *Construction Learning as a Complex Adaptive System*. Dodrecht: Springer.

Baicchi, Annalisa and Francisco José Ruiz de Mendoza Ibáñez. 2010. The cognitive grounding of illocutionary constructions within the theoretical perspective of the Lexical-Constructional Model.

Special Issue on "Cognition and the Brain in Language and Linguistics". *Textus* 23: 87–112.

Barthes, Roland. 1967. *Système de la mode*. Paris: Seuil.

Biscetti, Stefania and Annalisa Baicchi. 2019. Space oddity: What fashion terms can reveal about the English and Italian cognitive systems. *Culture, Fashion and Society Notebook* 5: 3–28.

Booij, Geert E. 2010. *Construction Morphology*. Oxford: Oxford University Press.

Catricalà, Maria. 2017. Fashion, journalism, and linguistic design: A case study of the wedding dresses. In Emanuela Mora and Marco Pedroni (eds.), *Fashion Tales. Feeding the Imaginary*. Bern: Peter Lang, 367–384.

Croft, William and Alan Cruse. 2004. *Cognitive Linguistics*. Cambridge: Cambridge University Press.

Fauconnier, Giles. 1985. *Mental Spaces: Aspects of Meaning Construction in Natural Language*. Cambridge: Cambridge University Press.

Fauconnier, Giles. 1994. *Mental Spaces*. Cambridge: Cambridge University Press.

Fillmore, Charles. 1982. "Frame semantics". In *Linguistics in the Morning Calm*. Selected Papers from SICOL-1981. Seoul: Hanshin Publishing Co., 111–137.

Geeraerts, Dirk, Stefan Grondalaers and Peter Bakema. 1994. *The Structure of Lexical Variation: Meaning, Naming and Context*. Berlin/New York: Walter de Gruyter.Glushko, Robert, Maglio Paul, Matlock Teenie, and Lawrence Barsalou. 2008. Categorization in the wild. *Trends in Cognitive Sciences* 12(4):129–35.

Goldberg, Adele Eve. 1995. *Constructions: A Construction Grammar Approach to Argument Structure*. Chicago: The University of Chicago Press.

Harnad, Stevan. 2005. "To cognize is to categorize: Cognition is categorization". In Henri Cohen and Claire Lefebvre (eds.), *Handbook of Categorization in Cognitive Science*. Amsterdam: Elsevier, 20–43.

Johnson, Mark. 2007. *The Meaning of the Body: Aesthetic of Human Understanding*. Chicago: The University of Chicago Press.

Kövecses, Zoltan. 2005. *Metaphor in Culture*. Cambridge, UK: Cambridge University Press.

Lakoff, George. 1987. *Women, Fire and Dangerous Things. What Categories Reveal about the Mind.* Chicago: The University of Chicago Press.

Lakoff, George and Mark Johnson. 1980. *Metaphors We Live By.* Chicago: Chicago University Press.

Lakoff, George and Mark Johnson. 1987. *Philosophy in the Flesh. The Embodied Mind and its Challenges to the Western Thought.* New York: Basic Books.

Langacker, Ronald. 2008. *Cognitive Grammar.* Oxford: Oxford University Press.

Lipka, Leonhard. 1992. *An Outline of English Lexicology. Lexical Structure, Word Semantics, and Word-Formation.* Max Niemeyer Verlag: Tübingen.

Mervis, Carolyn and Eleonor Rosch. 1981. Categorization of natural objects. *Annual Review of Psychology* 32: 89–115.

Radden, Günter, Klaus-Michael Kopcke, Thomas Berg, and Peter Siemund. 2007. *Aspects of Meaning Construction.* Amsterdam/Philadelphia: John Benjamins.

Rosch, Eleanor. 1977. "Human categorization". In N. Warren (ed.), *Studies in Cross-cultural Psychology.* London: Academic Press, vol. 1, 1–49.

Rosch, Eleanor and Carolyn Mervis. 1975. Family resemblances, Studies in the internal Structure of categories. *Cognitive Psychology* 7: 573–605.

Ruiz de Mendoza Ibáñez and Alicia Galera Masegosa. 2014. *Cognitive Modeling. A Linguistic Perspective.* Amsterdam/Philadelphia: John Benjamins.

Ruiz de Mendoza Ibáñez, Francisco José and Annalisa Baicchi. 2007. Illocutionary constructions: Cognitive motivation and linguistic realization. In Istvan Kecksek and Lawrence Horn (eds.), *Explorations in Pragmatics: Linguistic, Cognitive, and Intercultural Aspects.* Berlin/Boston: Mouton de Gruyter, 95–128.

Sharifian, Farzad. 2008. Distributed, emergent cultural cognition, conceptualisation, and language. In Roslyn Frank, René Dirven, Tom Ziemke and Enrique Bernardez (eds.), *Body, Language, and Mind: Vol. 2. Sociocultural Situatedness.* Berlin: Mouton de Gruyter, 109–136.

Sharifian, Farzad. 2011. *Cultural Conceptualisations and Language: Theoretical Framework and Applications*. Amsterdam/ Philadelphia: John Benjamins.

Sharifian, Farzad. 2015. "Cultural linguistics". In Farzad Sharifian (ed.), *The Routledge Handbook of Language and Culture*. London: Routledge, 473–492.

Sharifian, Farzad. 2017. *Cultural Linguistics*. Amsterdam/Philadelphia: John Benjamins.

Tortora, Phyllis and Sandra Keiser. 2014. *The Fairchild Books Dictionary of Fashion*. 4th edn. New York: Bloomsbury Publications.

Notes on Contributors

ANNALISA BAICCHI is Chair of English Linguistics at the Department of Modern Languages and Cultures, University of Genoa, Italy. Her research interests, both theoretical (e.g., Semantics, Cognitive Linguistics, Construction Grammar) and applied (e.g., lexicology, lexicography, translation), encompass the construction of meaning at the various levels of the linguistic and textual organization with the aim of identifying, also contrastively, the close-knit correlation between language structures and conceptual systems. She is a member of three International Projects for the development of a 'Semantic Theory of Meaning Construction' and she is research manager of the Italian computational implementation of an ontological multi-purpose and multi-lingual Natural Language Processing System. She has been Visiting Scholar at the St. Edmund Hall of the University of Oxford (UK), Visiting Scholar at the St. Catherine's College of the University of Oxford (UK), Visiting Professor at the University of Chicago (USA), Visiting Professor at the University of La Rioja (Spain), Visiting Faculty Professor at New York Eugene Nida School of Translation Studies (USA), Visiting Fellow at the University of Southampton (UK), and Visiting Professor at Fudan University of Shanghai (China). She serves as a peer referee for VQR ('Valutazione della Qualità della Ricerca', Anvur-ENQA), for National Research Projects, PRIN ('Progetti di Ricerca di Interesse Nazionale'), SIR (Scientific Independence of Young Researchers) and REPRISE (Register of Expert Peer Reviewers for Italian Scientific Evaluation) sponsored by Ministero dell'Istruzione, dell'Università e della Ricerca, and for International Research Projects, e.g., FWO ('Fonds Wetenschappelijk Onderzoek', Bruxelles), ANEP (Investigation, Development and Innovation, Ministry of Economy and Competition, Spain), DFF ('Det Frie Forskningsr.d') and FTP ('Forskningsr.d, Teknologi og Produktion') for the 'Dansk Ministeriet for Forskning, Innovation og Videregende Uddannelser' (Denmark), NSC: National Science Center (Poland); The British Academy: The UK's National Academy for the Humanities and Social Sciences (UK).

ISABEL BALTEIRO In addition to her wide experience as a researcher and as a lecturer, Isabel Balteiro has worked as a translator at the Student Advice and Information Centre of the University of Santiago de Compostela, Spain, and has more than three years' experience in management, a task she carried out at the General Directorate for Research and Development (I+D+i) of the Galician Regional Government. Isabel Balteiro has made a number of research stays in recognized centres and departments, including research at the universities of Oxford, Cambridge, Birmingham and Surray. She is a member of various scientific committees for scholarly journals, and is at present the Chief Editor of the Alicante Journal of English Studies. In addition to the Extraordinary Ph.D. Award from the University of Santiago de Compostela in 2007, she has received other awards and prizes, including the "English Language and Linguistics Award" granted by the Spanish Association for English and American Studies (AEDEAN) for her books on conversion or zero-derivation in English.

STEFANIA BISCETTI is tenured Assistant Professor of English Linguistics at the University of L'Aquila, Italy. She received her PhD in Linguistics (Institut für Sprachwissenschaft and Institut für Anglistik und Amerikanistik) from the University of Vienna (Austria) after graduating from the University of Pisa, Italy. Her research activity is mainly aimed at identifying the impact of culture (and ideology) on language use. Her research interests are therefore in the fields of language pragmatics (i.e., morphopragmatics, lexical and discourse pragmatics), stylistics, cognitive linguistics (conceptual metaphor theory) - approached both synchronically and diachronically - and specialised discourse. Her study on the history of the English intensifier *bloody* is mentioned in the Oxford English Dictionary and was used to update the correspondent entry. Her recently published monograph *Verbal Aggressiveness in English: A Speech Act Theory Approach* (2020) offers the first systematic investigation into aggressive language as distinct from impolite language.

SILVIA CACCHIANI is Associate Professor of English Language and Translation at the University of Modena and Reggio Emilia, Italy. She holds a PhD in English Language and Linguistics from the University of Pisa. She has published extensively on intensification and the semantics and pragmatics of phrasal constructs and complex words, applied aspects of ESP, and (specialized) lexicography. She has served as an anonymous referee for national and international journals, book series and conferences. She is currently working on the inclusion and lexicographic representation of complex word-formations in English and Italian general and specialized dictionaries of fashion and costume.

ELISA MATTIELLO is Associate Professor in English Language and Translation at the Universityof Pisa, Department of Philology, Literature and Linguistics. She holds a Ph.D. in English Linguistics from the same university, where she teaches courses of English Linguistics and ESP. Her main scientific interests are in the fields of English varieties, morphology, and specialised language. Her initial work was concerned with English slang, which is the topic of her monograph *An Introduction to English Slang: A Description of Its Morphology, Semantics and Sociology* (2008, Monza, Polimetrica). Her research has also produced the books *Extra-grammatical Morphology in English: Abbreviations, Blends, Reduplicatives, and Related Phenomena* (2013, Berlin/Boston, De Gruyter) and *The Popularisation of Business and Economic English in Online Newspapers* (2014/2015, Newcastle upon Tyne, CSP). Recently, her research has expanded in the direction of popularisation discourse, with the publication of various articles on digital genres of knowledge dissemination (e.g. politicians' Facebook profiles, scientific TED Talks, tourism websites) in national and international journals or collections. Her current research focuses on analogy in English word-formation, with various papers and the recent monograph *Analogy in Word-formation. A Study of English Neologisms and Occasionalisms* (2017, Berlin/Boston, De Gruyter).

ANNA ROMAGNUOLO is Associate Professor of English Language and Translation at the Department of Economics, Engineering, Society and Business Organization at the University of Tuscia in Viterbo, Italy. She is a licensed English and French Translator and Interpreter, licensed teacher of EFL, and teacher trainer. She has been teaching University courses of ESP and Translation into and from English since 2002. Her research interests include Translation Studies, Discourse Analysis,

Corpus Linguistics, and English Language Teaching. In particular, her interest in American Studies has led to several publications on Political Communication, Presidential Rhetoric and its Translation, among which her monograph *Transediting the President* (2014).

Louise Sylvester is Professor in English Language and teaches modules on the language of literary texts and the History of English. She was educated at the University of Leeds (BA Hons English Language and Literature) and King's College, London (MA Literature and Language Before 1525; PhD Historical Semantics). She was AHRB/HEFCE Research Fellow at King's College, London and taught at the University of Manchester and the University of Central England in Birmingham. She was Co-Investigator on the AHRC-funded five-year project, The Lexis of Cloth and Clothing in Britain c.700–1450: Origins, Identification, Contexts and Change; Principal Investigator on the Leverhulme Trust-funded three-year project The Vocabulary of Medieval Dress and Textiles in Unpublished Sources; Co-Investigator (and later PI) on the Leverhulme-funded three-year project A Bilingual Thesaurus; Principal Investigator on a one-year AHRC-funded project Lexis of Cloth and Clothing: the medieval Royal Wardrobe accounts; Co-Investigator on the AHRC-funded Medieval English in a Multilingual Context network; Principal Investigator on the Leverhulme-funded three-year project Technical language and semantic shift in Middle English. Her research is focused on the vocabulary in use in medieval England. Her most recent papers have concerned lexical choices across text types within the multilingual textual culture of medieval Britain.

Linguistic Insights

Studies in Language and Communication

This series aims to promote specialist language studies in the fields of linguistic theory and applied linguistics, by publishing volumes that focus on specific aspects of language use in one or several languages and provide valuable insights into language and communication research. A cross-disciplinary approach is favoured and most European languages are accepted.

The series includes two types of books:

- Monographs – featuring in-depth studies on special aspects of language theory, language analysis or language teaching.
- Collected papers – assembling papers from workshops, conferences or symposia.

Each volume of the series is subjected to a double peer-reviewing process.

Vol. 1   Maurizio Gotti & Marina Dossena (eds)
          Modality in Specialized Texts. Selected Papers of the 1st CERLIS Conference.
          421 pages. 2001. ISBN 3-906767-10-8 · US-ISBN 0-8204-5340-4

Vol. 2   Giuseppina Cortese & Philip Riley (eds)
          Domain-specific English. Textual Practices across Communities
          and Classrooms.
          420 pages. 2002. ISBN 3-906768-98-8 · US-ISBN 0-8204-5884-8

Vol. 3   Maurizio Gotti, Dorothee Heller & Marina Dossena (eds)
          Conflict and Negotiation in Specialized Texts. Selected Papers
          of the 2nd CERLIS Conference.
          470 pages. 2002. ISBN 3-906769-12-7 · US-ISBN 0-8204-5887-2

Vol. 4   Maurizio Gotti, Marina Dossena, Richard Dury, Roberta Facchinetti & Maria Lima
          Variation in Central Modals. A Repertoire of Forms and Types of Usage
          in Middle English and Early Modern English.
          364 pages. 2002. ISBN 3-906769-84-4 · US-ISBN 0-8204-5898-8

Editorial address:

Prof. Maurizio Gotti,   Università di Bergamo, Dipartimento di Lingue, Letterature e Culture
Emeritus Professor   Straniere Piazza Rosate 2, 24129 Bergamo, Italy
                         Fax: +39 035 2052789, E-Mail: m.gotti@unibg.it

Vol. 102   Nuria Edo Marzá
            The Specialised Lexicographical Approach. A Step further in Dictionary-making.
            316 pages. 2009. ISBN 978-3-0343-0043-8

Vol. 103   Carlos Prado-Alonso, Lidia Gómez-García, Iria Pastor-Gómez &
            David Tizón-Couto (eds)
            New Trends and Methodologies in Applied English Language Research.
            Diachronic, Diatopic and Contrastive Studies.
            348 pages. 2009. ISBN 978-3-0343-0046-9

Vol. 104   Françoise Salager-Meyer & Beverly A. Lewin
            Crossed Words. Criticism in Scholarly Writing?
            371 pages. 2011. ISBN 978-3-0343-0049-0.

Vol. 105   Javier Ruano-García
            Early Modern Northern English Lexis. A Literary Corpus-Based Study.
            611 pages. 2010. ISBN 978-3-0343-0058-2

Vol. 106   Rafael Monroy-Casas
            Systems for the Phonetic Transcription of English. Theory and Texts.
            280 pages. 2011. ISBN 978-3-0343-0059-9

Vol. 107   Nicola T. Owtram
            The Pragmatics of Academic Writing.
            A Relevance Approach to the Analysis of Research Article Introductions.
            311 pages. 2009. ISBN 978-3-0343-0060-5

Vol. 108   Yolanda Ruiz de Zarobe, Juan Manuel Sierra &
            Francisco Gallardo del Puerto (eds)
            Content and Foreign Language Integrated Learning.
            Contributions to Multilingualism in European Contexts
            343 pages. 2011. ISBN 978-3-0343-0074-2

Vol. 109   Ángeles Linde López & Rosalía Crespo Jiménez (eds)
            Professional English in the European context. The EHEA challenge.
            374 pages. 2010. ISBN 978-3-0343-0088-9

Vol. 110   Rosalía Rodríguez-Vázquez
            The Rhythm of Speech, Verse and Vocal Music. A New Theory.
            394 pages. 2010. ISBN 978-3-0343-0309-5

Vol. 111   Anastasios Tsangalidis & Roberta Facchinetti (eds)
            Studies on English Modality. In Honour of Frank Palmer.
            392 pages. 2009. ISBN 978-3-0343-0310-1

Vol. 112   Jing Huang
            Autonomy, Agency and Identity in Foreign Language Learning and Teaching.
            400 pages. 2013. ISBN 978-3-0343-0370-5

Vol. 113   Mihhail Lotman & Maria-Kristiina Lotman (eds)
            Frontiers in Comparative Prosody. In memoriam: Mikhail Gasparov.
            426 pages. 2011. ISBN 978-3-0343-0373-6

Vol. 114   Merja Kytö, John Scahill & Harumi Tanabe (eds)
            Language Change and Variation from Old English to Late Modern English.
            A Festschrift for Minoji Akimoto
            422 pages. 2010. ISBN 978-3-0343-0372-9

Vol. 115   Giuliana Garzone & Paola Catenaccio (eds)
            Identities across Media and Modes. Discursive Perspectives.
            379 pages. 2009. ISBN 978-3-0343-0386-6

Vol. 144   Margrethe Petersen & Jan Engberg (eds)
             Current Trends in LSP Research. Aims and Methods.
             323 pages. 2011. ISBN 978-3-0343-1054-3

Vol. 145   David Tizón-Couto, Beatriz Tizón-Couto, Iria Pastor-Gómez & Paula Rodríguez-Puente (eds)
             New Trends and Methodologies in Applied English Language Research II.
             Studies in Language Variation, Meaning and Learning.
             283 pages. 2012. ISBN 978-3-0343-1061-1

Vol. 146   Rita Salvi & Hiromasa Tanaka (eds)
             Intercultural Interactions in Business and Management.
             306 pages. 2011. ISBN 978-3-0343-1039-0

Vol. 147   Francesco Straniero Sergio & Caterina Falbo (eds)
             Breaking Ground in Corpus-based Interpreting Studies.
             254 pages. 2012. ISBN 978-3-0343-1071-0

Vol. 148   Forthcoming.

Vol. 149   Vijay K. Bhatia & Paola Evangelisti Allori (eds)
             Discourse and Identity in the Professions. Legal, Corporate and Institutional Citizenship.
             352 pages. 2011. ISBN 978-3-0343-1079-6

Vol. 150   Maurizio Gotti (ed.)
             Academic Identity Traits. A Corpus-Based Investigation.
             363 pages. 2012. ISBN 978-3-0343-1141-0

Vol. 151   Priscilla Heynderickx, Sylvain Dieltjens, Geert Jacobs, Paul Gillaerts &
             Elizabeth de Groot (eds)
             The Language Factor in International Business.
             New Perspectives on Research, Teaching and Practice.
             320 pages. 2012. ISBN 978-3-0343-1090-1

Vol. 152   Paul Gillaerts, Elizabeth de Groot, Sylvain Dieltjens, Priscilla Heynderickx &
             Geert Jacobs (eds)
             Researching Discourse in Business Genres. Cases and Corpora.
             215 pages. 2012. ISBN 978-3-0343-1092-5

Vol. 153   Yongyan Zheng
             Dynamic Vocabulary Development in a Foreign Language.
             262 pages. 2012. ISBN 978-3-0343-1106-9

Vol. 154   Carmen Argondizzo (ed.)
             Creativity and Innovation in Language Education.
             357 pages. 2012. ISBN 978-3-0343-1080-2

Vol. 155   David Hirsh (ed.)
             Current Perspectives in Second Language Vocabulary Research.
             180 pages. 2012. ISBN 978-3-0343-1108-3

Vol. 156   Seiji Shinkawa
             Unhistorical Gender Assignment in Lahamon's *Brut*. A Case Study of a Late Stage
             in the Development of Grammatical Gender toward its Ultimate Loss.
             186 pages. 2012. ISBN 978-3-0343-1124-3

Vol. 157   Yeonkwon Jung
             Basics of Organizational Writing: A Critical Reading Approach.
             151 pages. 2014. ISBN 978-3-0343-1137-3.

Vol. 293   Annalisa Baicchi / Stefania Biscetti (eds.)
The Language of Fashion. Linguistic, Cognitive, and Cultural Insights
190 pages. 2022. 978-3-0343-4428-9